The Ultimate Guide to West Michigan Lighthouses

JERRY ROACH

FOREWORD BY
TERRY PEPPER

The Ultimate Guide To

West Michigan Lighthouses

The Ultimate Guide To

West Michigan Lighthouses

Text: Jerry Roach

Directions: Jerry and Barb Roach

Photographs: Jerry and Barb Roach

Bugs Publishing LLC

Contents

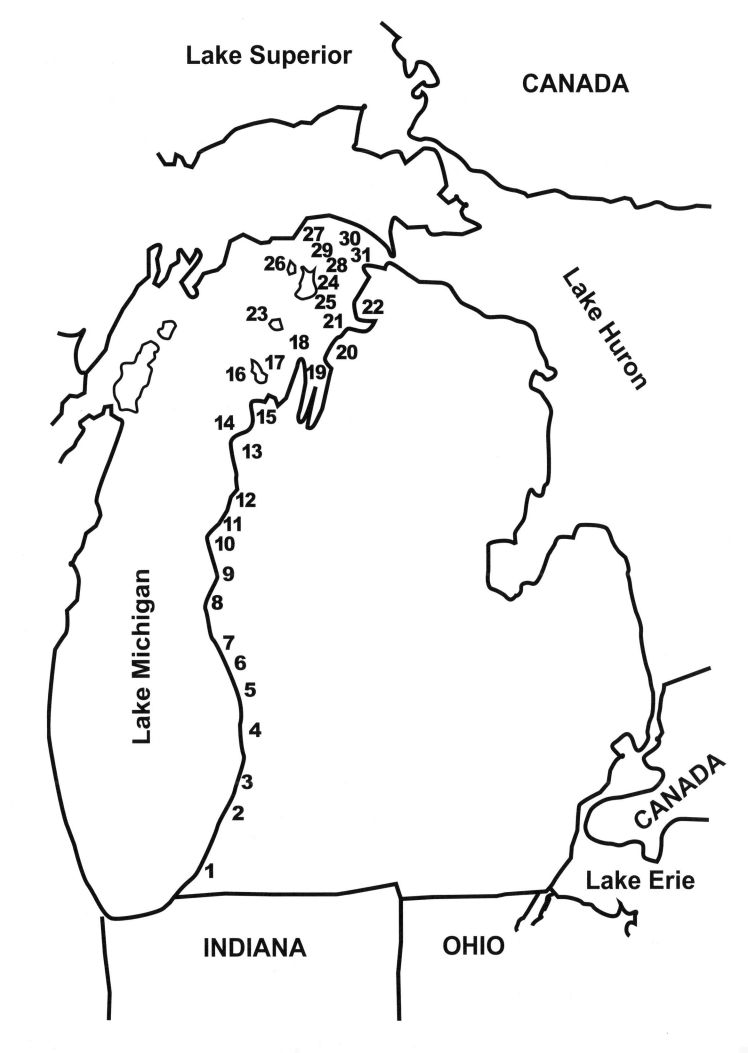

Lake Superior

CANADA

Lake Huron

Lake Michigan

27 30
29 31
26 28
24
25   22
23 21
18   20
16 17 19

14 15
13

12
11
10
9
8
7
6
5
4
3
2
1

INDIANA   OHIO

CANADA

Lake Erie

Acknowledgments

We would be remiss if we did not take the time to thank the many people that helped in some way with either our web site or our book. During our travels we have made many new friends and explored countless sites. Had these folks not given their time and effort, or lent their support, we may not have realized the final project. Barb and I would like to devote this page in our book to personally thank each and every one of you.

To Kristofer Engelhardt, thanks for the seed you planted at our first self-publishing workshop.

Instructors Dan Symons and Beth Tyburski at the Skill Center, Saginaw Metal Castings, for your computer and photo editing help.

Computer skills taught by Denise Koets, at the Bendle/Carmen – Ainsworth Community Education Center.

Tony Gray at InTouch Communications, for getting the web site off the ground.

Jeff Davis at Pro look Ink, our web designer.

Mike Miller at the Owosso Wal-Mart, our photo-finish guru.

Everett Jones and Kristy Edgerton, great people at the Ritz Camera Store located in the Genesse Valley Mall.

Randy Fowler and the gang at Creek Auto Service, they kept the truck on the road.

To all the folks at AAA, thanks for the maps, directions, and the travel discounts.

Ron Arms, he did a great job updating our computer.

Patty Broderick, she is our typing and software genius.

Joshua and Zachary Roach, Jamie Goodrich, they often kept watch over our four legged children when they couldn't go with us.

Dr. Rangi D.V.M and the staff at Pinecrest Animal Hospital, they take great care of our four legged children and sometimes watch them when we travel.

Patricia A. Broderick, thanks for watching Candy and for the monetary support.

Becky Landris from the Durand School District, she did a fine job proofreading our documents.

Grandma Broderick provided us with many reference articles.

Capt. Dan Higdon of Island Hopper Charters, we had a great time exploring the islands of Lake Michigan.

Rick and Rita Feeley, our friends that traveled, and split the cost, of our Lake Michigan adventure.

The Brothers Inn on Beaver Island, thanks for the hospitality and use of your van.

Roland Cull, you will not find a better tour guide on Beaver Island.

Heather Coselman, Janet Redford, and the gang at DeLux Monogramming and Screen Printing in Durand, they do great work.

Scott McCullum, he is the man that keeps our books straight.

Manitou Island Transit, they provided us with safe passage to Manitou Island and Manitou Reef.

Shepler's Ferry, we rode comfortably to photograph many lights with their crew.

Megan and David at the Petoskey Area Chamber of Commerce went out of their way to help us when we were in the area.

Mike Esposito at the Irish Boat Shop, thanks for your help.

Kristie DeBeck, she was a great guide when visiting Harbor Springs.

Richard Baldwin, writer and lecturer, for providing additional inspiration to self-publish and helping with many questions.

Gala White and The Shiawassee Scribblers, they hosted the workshop on self-publishing.

Sarah Thomas, she did a great job with our cover design.

Sandy Planisek, we appreciate your support with our project.

Terry Pepper, we appreciate your help and hard work.

Thank you Ellison and Edith Roach for your support.

Thank you Betsie, Mary Jane, Lillian, and the gang at Celia's by the Bay in Frankfort.
Thank you to all the team members at Target 350 on Miller Rd., Flint.

Our acknowledgments would not be complete if we fail to mention all the men and women, along with their families, that braved the rough conditions to tend the many Michigan lighthouses. We also would like to thank the men and women of the United States Coast Guard that accepted the responsibility of the lights since 1939. Most of all, we would like to thank the numerous preservation and restoration groups that have taken it upon themselves to preserve these wonderful pieces of history. Groups like the Great Lakes Lighthouse Keepers Association, which we are members, need your support. We urge you to join a group associated with your favorite light so that these beacons can shine forever.

The author and publisher do not accept any liability or responsibility for loss or damage, real or implied, which may be represented as a result of reading and/or use of this book. Although the author and publisher have exhaustively researched all sources to ensure the accuracy and completeness of the information contained in this book, we assume no responsibility for errors, inaccuracies, omissions or any inconsistency herein. Any slights of people or organizations are unintentional. Readers should use their own judgment when using this book. Changes in road names may occur, and mileage notations were made as carefully and exact as possible. All events and attractions, at the time of publication, have historically occurred or have been in existence for a number of years.

Bugs Publishing LLC
8524 Monroe Rd.
Durand, Michigan 48429

ISBN Number 0 – 9747977 – 0 – 7

Printed in the United States of America

1st Printing 2005
2nd Printing 2006

Preface

Michigan is truly the Great Lakes State, with two peninsulas surrounded by thousands of acres of fresh water. As civilization quickly moved from the east, Michigan was a natural draw with its abundance of natural resources. Communities quickly grew and expanded throughout the state. As commerce spread from sources such as lumber, iron ore, copper, the need for adequate harbors was obvious. Ship traffic in the early days was an adventure of its own. There were numerous reefs and shoals that claimed many of the pioneering vessels.

It is said that technology is a wonderful thing. Ten years ago most of us did not own a cell phone. Today however, leave the phone at home and we don't know how we got along without one. With the invention of sonar, radar, and GPS, many of us could not relate to the perils that rest below the surface of the water.

Other parts of the world knew of the importance of lighthouses to show the way for ships at sea. The U.S. Lighthouse Service was formed in 1789 to perform the task of building and manning lights at dangerous locations. Fort Gratiot was the first light established on the Michigan shoreline in 1825. As development and ship traffic increased, others soon followed. There have been many advances in the source of light from the lighthouses as well. The first light in St. Joseph was said to be nothing more than lanterns in the windows of a home near the shoreline. In the beginning the lights burned whale oil. As technology advanced, lighthouses were converted to kerosene or acetylene, which could burn brighter and required less maintenance.

Even with the new technology ships continued to wreck. As a result, two new solutions arrived to aid in navigation. In mid 1800's the Fresnel lens improved the distance and brightness of each light. The light at Waugoshance Shoal was the first light in Michigan to use the Fresnel lens. A few years later, the U.S. Life Saving Service was formed to assist and rescue any ship that may be in need. However, the next round of technological improvements would spell the end for many lighthouses, and light keepers around the state.

Electricity began arriving at lighthouses across the region. With the implementation of electricity the lighthouses could be automated. Automation in turn spelled the end for the light keepers. St. Helena became the first victim to lose its keeper, and in 1983, Pt. Betsie became the last. The Life Saving Service also fell victim to technology. Powerboats and helicopters were more effective when lives needed to be saved.

Today, the lighthouses face a whole new challenge. As the Coast Guard assumed control of the lights in 1939, they were in charge of the conversion of the lights. Once the conversion was complete, the lighthouses were abandoned. Thoughtless individuals soon took it upon themselves to wreak havoc on these majestic pieces of history. Many lights were destroyed. The decision was soon made to sell the lights as a cost cutting measure.

Thankfully, numerous historical societies, and citizens interested in preservation, have taken it upon themselves to manage lighthouses on this list. Other groups have adopted lights in their region and began the task of restoration to preserve history for generations to come. This is a daunting task. The cost involved, and the man-hours required to repair, or sometimes to simply contain the lights current status, can be overwhelming.

This is where you and I come in. We have dedicated our web site, www.lighthousecentral.com, and a portion of each Internet sale, to preservation and restoration groups throughout the United States. We also help promote merchandise and events that any group may choose to offer. While this may seem noble, the real need is for volunteers. We can no longer sit by and hope others will step up to the plate. If we all choose not to participate, there may be many more of these lights that will be extinguished forever.

Foreword

I first met Jerry and Barb during a Fall ATV trip to Fourteen Mile Point Lighthouse, and was immediately impressed with the eagerness and sincerity with which they approached their discovery of this magnificent and difficult to visit lighthouse.

In this first volume of their planned series of regional guides to Michigan lighthouses, Jerry and Barb provide a combination of information previously unavailable to the lighthouse aficionado.

While there are other books which provide photographs and directions, this book stands out from the crowd by giving a richer sense of the history of each light station combined with detailed driving instructions from multiple directions, recommended scenic drives and a listing of interesting annual events in the area to include when planning a lighthouse tour.

Anyone planning on experiencing the majesty of Michigan's West Coast lights first-hand will be well served by taking this book along to serve as your guide.

Terry Pepper

__Introduction__

Like you, lighthouses have been a fascination for us as long as we can remember. In fact, it was while we were dating that we realized lighthouses were a common interest. At the beginning of every year, Barb and I enjoy formulating our plans, and plotting the best use of our time to absorb the wonders of the Great Lakes and the beautiful lighthouses. The idea for this book came about on one of our adventures exploring lighthouses. On this day, we had an extremely hard time finding the Old Presque Isle Lighthouse. Eventually we found the light, took some photographs, and then left to visit a different light. While on our way to visit the next light on our list, we decided to write a book on Michigan Lighthouses.

There are many great books in print today about the lights of Michigan. Our challenge was to arrive at an idea that would offer something not yet seen in any other lighthouse books. In this book, you will find many similar concepts, but a few new twists as well. In our book, we will show photographs, and provide some history. The new wrinkle is to provide three different types of directions to each light, and inform our readers of points of interest in the area surrounding the light.

Starting at St. Joseph North Pier Light, in addition to a direct route to each light, the GPS Waypoints and a scenic route are given. The scenic route provides an alternate route from light to light using the side roads. All roads are paved. These routes allow the traveler a scenic and peaceful journey through the great state of Michigan. We found many new sites that we never would have seen had we stayed on the highway.

Another new element our book provides is an avenue to explore the communities surrounding each light. Each light lists museums, points of interest, and a calendar of annual fairs, festivals, and events. The idea for this addition to the book came to us when the Venetian Festival was in full swing as we arrived to photograph the St. Joseph Pier Light.

Barb and I have had a great experience traveling our state while visiting the lights. We hope you use this book to expand and make new memories along your own journeys to each light. Take your time, and happy lighthouse hunting.

Jerry and Barb Roach

1.) St. Joseph Pier Lights

The lights in St. Joseph are positioned along the north breakwall were the St. Joseph River empties into Lake Michigan. Ships arrived on a regular basis as early as the 1800's. Navigating in inclement weather, as well as in the dark, was a risky proposition. The light in St. Joseph was the first one to be built in Michigan on the shores of Lake Michigan. The city of St. Joseph has had a total of four lights built at the river mouth. The first light was in reality nothing more than lanterns placed in the windows of a home built near the shore. Therefore, records indicate that a light was established in St. Joseph in 1832. The first lighthouse as we know them today, was built on a hill overlooking the harbor in 1859. This light remained faithful until it was deactivated in 1924. Sadly, this lighthouse was torn down in 1955 to make way for a parking lot. In 1906, the pier along the river was extended 1,000 feet, and the outer pier light began its service to navigation. The outer light's tower stands 35 feet tall and still uses a fifth order Fresnel lens. One year later, the inner pier light was added to form a range light system with the outer pier light. The inner pier light stands 57 feet tall. The inner pier light has the appearance of an actual lighthouse. Today, this tower is powered by a fourth order Fresnel lens. A catwalk that was used to service the lights when the seas became hostile connects the two lights.

Direct Route:

Take exit 33 from I-94 go 4.9 miles. Turn right on M-63 go 0.3 miles. Turn right on Edgewater go 0.1 mile. Turn left on Whitman go 0.3 miles. Turn right on Upton go 0.2 miles. Turn left on Marina go 0.3 miles. Turn left on Ridgeway go 0.1 mile. Turn right into Tiscornia Park.

GPS Waypoints:

42° 06.97N
086° 29.653W

Attractions and Events

Museums:

Fort Miami Heritage Society of Michigan
www.fortmiani.org
269-983-1191

Krasl Art Center
www.krasl.org
616-983-0271

Curious Kids Museum
www.curiouskidsmusem.org
269-983-2543

Morton House Museum
269-429-8243

Points of Interest:

Hidden Pointe Mini Golf
269-926-1358

Box Factory for the Arts
269-983-3688

Tabor Hill Winery
269-422-1165

Nature Center:

Sarett Nature Center
www.sarett.com
269-927-4832

Fairs & Festivals:

April
International Food Fair
800-253-2874
Blossom Time Festival
269-926-7397
Annual Easter Egg Hunt

May
Memorial Day Parade
Kite Festival
269-657-5395

July
Krasl Art Fair
www.krasl.org
Eau Claire Cherry Festival
www.eauclairecherryfest.org
Venetian Festival
www.venetian.org
Berrien Springs Pickle Fest
269-449-2910

August
Berrien County Youth Fair
www.bcyf.org

September
TriState Regatta/Sailing Festival
269-982-0032
Berrien Springs Jazz Festival
269-471-1202

October
Harvest Festival
269-982-0032
Halloween Festival
269-982-0032

November
Luminary Festival
269-982-0032

Contacts:

Cornerstone Chamber of Commerce
www.cstonealliance.org
269-925-6100

St. Joseph Today
www.sjtoday.org
269-985-1111

2.) South Haven Pier Light

The lumber industry sprouted in the South Haven area around the 1850's. The Black River was a natural passageway for the retrieval of the logs for the lumber companies. In 1866 a large sawmill was built, thereby increasing the number of ships entering the area. As a result, it was only a matter of time before it became necessary to build some type of navigational aid. Construction of a lighthouse began in South Haven in 1870. However, because of a loss of funds, the light was not finished until 1872. The first tower and catwalk built were made of wood. In 1901, the pier was extended and the light was repositioned at its end. The wooden tower served faithfully until 1903 when the current 35 – foot steel tower was erected. The fifth order Fresnel lens was moved from the wooden tower to the new steel tower. Later, in 1913, the pier was once again extended and the tower was moved to its current location. In 1916, a 52 – foot tall light was constructed to the rear of the first light. Together, the two lights would function as range lights. At some undocumented date, the range light system was abandoned and the wooden catwalk converted to steel. The keeper's dwelling was donated to the city of South Haven in August of 2000. The Michigan Maritime Museum intends to renovate the building and use it as a reference library.

Scenic Route:

From St. Joseph, return to Upton turn left. Go 0.3 miles to Momany turn right. Go 0.3 miles to M-63 turn left. Go 22 miles to Business Rt. 196 turn left. (M-63 becomes Blue Star Highway.) Go 1.5 miles to Phoenix turn left. Go 0.6 miles to South Beach parking area. (Phoenix becomes Water St.)

GPS Waypoints:

42° 24. 081N
086° 17.280W

Direct Route:

Take exit 20 off I-196, Business Rt. 196 go west. No turns, BR-196 becomes Phoenix and then Water St. Follow signs to South Beach.

Attractions and Events

Museums:
> *Michigan Maritime Museum*
>> www.michiganmaritimemuseum.org
>> 269-637-8078
> *Liberty Hyde Bailey Museum*
>> 269-637-3251

Points of Interest:
> *U.S. Coast Guard Life Saving Service Exhibit*
>> 800-747-3810, 269-637-8078
> *Apple Ridge Farm*
>> 269-674-4222
> *Creative Sparks*
>> 269-637-0289
> *Fideland Fun Park*
>> 269-637-3123

Nature Centers:
> *Love Creek Nature Center*
>> 269-471-2617

Fairs & Festivals:
> **February**
>> **Ice Breaker Festival**
> **June**
>> **Harbor Fest**
>> 800-SO-HAVEN
>> **Annual Art Fair**
> **July**
>> **Classic Boat Show**
>> 800-747-3810
>> **Festival of Cars**
>> 800-SO-HAVEN
>> **Van Buren County Youth Fair**
>> 269-621-0238
> **August**
>> **Blueberry Festival**
>> 800-SO-HAVEN
>> **Berrien County Youth Fair**
>> 269-473-4251
>> **Annual All Crafts Fair**
>> 269-637-5252
> **September**
>> **Antique Engine & Tractor Show**
>> 269-639-2010
> **October**
>> **Bangor Apple Fest**

Contacts:
> **South Haven Chamber of Commerce**
>> www.southhavenmi.com
>> 269-637-5171
>
> **LakeShore Convention & Visitors Bureau**
>> www.southhaven.org
>> 800-SO-HAVEN

3.) Kalamazoo River Light

As with many of the early settlements, the logging industry played a major role in the growth of the city of Saugatuck. As the town grew, the river was used more extensively. In 1839, the first light was constructed along the banks of the Kalamazoo River. A sixth order Fresnel lens was installed in the light in 1856. The new Fresnel lens replaced lanterns that had been used as the source of light. Sand around the lighthouse began to blow away because of a lack of trees. Due to this erosion, in 1858 the lighthouse collapsed. In 1859, a new site was chosen and work crews finished the new lighthouse, complete with a fifth order Fresnel lens. Because of its location away from the pier, the lens was moved from the lighthouse to the pier in 1876. A problem arose in 1892 as a steamer slammed into the pier light and damaged it severely. As a result, the lens was moved back to the lighthouse. Many changes occurred through the years for the Kalamazoo Light, and the blowing sand continued to raise havoc. Once the installation of lights on the north and south piers were completed in 1914, the lighthouse was officially deactivated in 1915. In 1937, the lighthouse was sold to a private owner. No stranger to adversity however, the lighthouse once again suffered as it was destroyed by a tornado in 1956. The lighthouse look – a – like that is now at the entrance to the Kalamazoo River was built with some materials from the original light and is a private home.

Scenic Route:

From South Haven return 1.3 miles to BR-196 and Blue Star Hwy junction turn left. Go 17.6 miles turn left on Center. Go 0.4 miles turn right on Ferry. Go 1.2 miles turn left on Perryman. Go 0.5 miles to Oval Beach parking. There is a parking fee. Structure is at the north end of the parking area. Follow the trails through the dunes. Property is private, stay behind fence.

GPS Waypoints:

42° 39.903N
086° 12.780W

Direct Route:

Take exit 36 from US 31 / I-196. Take Blue Star Hwy north turn left on Center at first stoplight. Go 0.4 miles turn right on Ferry. Go 1.2 miles turn left on Perryman. Go 0.5 miles to Oval Beach parking area. Structure is at the north end of the parking area. Follow the trails through the dunes. The property is private, stay behind the fence.

Attractions and Events

Museums:
> *Sloan Museum*
>> 269-857-2107
>
> *S.S. Keewatin Maritime Museum*

Points of Interest:
> *Star of Saugatuck*
>> 269-857-4261
>
> *Saugatuck Dune Rides*
>> www.saugatuckdunerides.com
>
> *Mt. Baldhead*
>
> *Peterson's Mill*
>
> *Crane's Corn Maze*
>> 269-561-8651

Fairs & Festivals:
> **February**
>> **Food, Wine & All That Jazz**
>> 800-647-6023
>
> **March**
>> **Mardi Gras Parade**
>> 269-857-1438
>
> **May**
>> **Tulip Time Festival**
>> 269-396-4221
>> **Memorial Day Parade**
>
> **June**
>> **Annual Arts & Crafts Fair**
>> 269-857-1701
>> **Waterfront Film Festival**
>> www.waterfrontfilm.com
>
> **July**
>> **Invitational Juried Art Fair**
>> 269-857-1701
>> **Harbor Days & Venetian Nights**
>> 269-857-1701
>> **4th of July Celebration**
>
> **September**
>> **Allegan County Fair**
>> www.allegancountyfair.org
>> **Blue Star Bridge Walk**
>> 269-857-1701
>> **Heritage Festival**
>> www.sdhistory.accn.org
>
> **October**
>> **Douglas October Fest**
>> **Goose Festival**
>> 269-561-5013
>> **Halloween Festival**
>> 269-857-1701

Contacts:

Saugatuck-Douglas Convention & Visitors Bureau
> www.saugatuck.com

4.) Holland Harbor Lighthouse

Dutch settlers began arriving in the Holland area around 1847. Not long after, it became apparent that if ships could enter Lake Matawa from Lake Michigan, it would stimulate growth. In the beginning, the Federal Government refused to allocate any funds for harbor improvements. Determined to improve navigational quality, the town folk decided to dig the channel themselves. In 1859, they accomplished that goal. Upon completion, Congress allocated the funds to build a pier light, and it was shown for the first time in 1872. The original light resembled the light in Charlevoix, and included a wooden catwalk to protect the keepers from rough seas. Later, in 1890, a light was constructed at the outer edge of the pier so the lights could function as range lights. The original wooden structure would prove to be no match for rough Lake Michigan seas. The wooden structures were torn down and replaced by a steel tower. The pier ends were altered in 1916 and a 27 – foot high tower was built to form range lights. These lights finally became powered by electricity in 1932. Sometime in 1956 the Coast Guard painted the rear building, which comprised the light and fog signal building, bright red. Navigators are well aware that red is on the right when returning to harbor, and the Holland Light is on the south pier. Obviously, it was as a result of this paint job that the light is called "Big Red." The people of Holland saved the light from ruin in 1970.

Scenic Route:

From Oval Beach return to Blue Star Hwy turn left. Go 7.2 miles to stop sign turn left. (This is still Blue Star Hwy.) Go 2.5 miles to 64th St. turn right. Go 0.9 miles to Lincoln turn left. Go 2.1 miles jog left on State. (Stay in right lane at this light, left lane is for a sharp left turn.) Go 1.1 miles jog right on River. Go 1.5 miles turn left on Douglas. Go 5.8 miles to Holland State Park.

GPS Waypoints:

42° 46.432N
086° 12.742W

Direct Route:

Exit US-31 at Business Rt. 31 and go west 1.3 miles to River. Turn right go 1 mile to Douglas. Turn left go 5.8 miles to Holland State Park.

Attractions and Events

Museums:
    Cappon House
        www.hollandmuseum.org
    Windmill Island
        www.windmillisland.org
    Holland Museum
        www.hollandmuseum.org

Points of Interest:
    Dutch Village Theme Park
        www.dutchvillage.com
    Veldheer Tulip Gardens
        www.veldheertulip.com
    Deklomp Wooden Shoe & Delft Factory
        616-399-1803

Nature Center:
    DeGraff Nature Center
        616-396-2739

Fairs & Festivals:
May
    Tulip Time Festival
    www.tuliptime.org
    Annual Memorial Day Parade
July
    Ottawa County Fair
    616-399-4904
    Annual 4th of July Fireworks
September
    Pumpkin Festival
October
    Tulipanes Latino Art & Film
    www.tlaff.org
November
    Dutch Winter Fest
    800-509-1299
December
    Ice Sculpting Contest

Contacts:
    Holland Chamber of Commerce
        www.holland-chamber.org
        616-392-2389

    Holland Area Convention & Visitors
        www.holland.org
        800-506-1299

5.) Grand Haven Pier Lights

In all, Grand Haven has had five different lights guiding vessels to its harbor. The original lighthouse was built in 1838 and was simplistic at best. As the population and the shipping grew, it became necessary to build a true lighthouse. So, in 1839, the first actual lighthouse was built. Soon however, it became apparent that a change was necessary. The light was displayed too low to be seen and needed to be elevated. Eventually, in 1854, a lighthouse was built higher, above the harbor. As improvements were made in the channel, a fog signal building was constructed on the south pier in 1875. Over the years work continued on the south pier, and a 60 – foot tower light was installed in 1881. Finally, in 1893, the construction and extension improvements were completed, bringing the pier to the current length. In 1907, the current 51 – foot inner light was built. The new light replaced the tower that was erected in 1881. As it turns out, renovations were not complete. In 1909, the inner light was moved closer to shore so that it could serve together with the outer light as range lights. The catwalk that connects both lights to the shore was built in 1922. It is interesting to note that in 1986, the Coast Guard had planned to remove the catwalk for fear of liability. A group called "Save the Catwalk Committee," stepped in and raised money for its restoration. In addition to saving the catwalk, the committee installed lights the length of the entire pier. These lights were displayed for the first time in 1988.

Scenic Route:

From Holland leave parking area and go 0.9 miles to 168th Ave turn left. Go 0.3 miles turn left on Lakeshore. Go 8.3 miles to stop sign turn left. Go 17.2 miles to Washington turn left. Go 0.4 miles to Harbor turn left. Go 1.1 miles to State Park parking. (Lakeshore will turn into Sheldon and then 5th St., no turns.)

GPS Waypoints:

43° 03.417N
086° 15.367W

Direct Route:

From US-31 turn west on Franklin and go 0.8 miles. Turn left on Harbor Dr. Go 0.9 miles to State Park parking.

Attractions and Events

Museums:
> *Tricities Historical Museum*
>> 616-842-0700
> *Coopersville Farm Museum*
>> 616-987-8555

Points of Interest:
> *Musical Fountain*
>> 616-842-4910
> *Harbor Steamer*
>> 616-842-8950
> *The Grand Lady Riverboat*
>> 616-457-4837

Fairs & Festivals:
> May
>> **Great Lakes Kite Festival**
>> www.mackite.com
>> **Annual Grand Quacker Duck Race**
>> **Memorial Day Festivities**
> June
>> **Heritage Festival**
>> 800-303-4088
>> **Fest of the Strawberry Moon**
>> **Queen's Cup Race**
>> **Annual Sand Sculpture Contest**
> July
>> **Ottawa County Fair**
>> 616-399-4904
>> **Coast Guard Festival**
>> 888-207-2434
>> **Annual Wheels of Grand Haven Car Show**
>> **Annual Flower Show**
> September
>> **Salmon & Song Fest**
> December
>> **Annual Christmas Parade**

Contacts:

Grand Haven Chamber of Commerce
> www.grandhavenchamber.org
> 616-842-4910

Grand Haven/Spring Lake Area Visitors Bureau
> 800-303-4088

6.) Muskegon South Pier Light

The first lighthouse to appear in the Muskegon area was actually a structure that was built on shore. The channel that connects Muskegon Lake to Lake Michigan was at this time undeveloped. This makeshift lighthouse was in reality nothing more than the keeper's home with a light on the roof. This lighthouse was established in 1851. With an increase in shipping, and the population of Muskegon on the rise, work on the harbor and pier were desperately needed. The Army Corps of Engineers arrived and began the process of improving and lengthening the pier. They finished the improvements in 1902. With the new pier finished, it was decided that the shore light was no longer useful. As a result, plans began for a light to be placed at the end of the pier. In 1903, the current 53 – foot cast iron tower was built. The source of light was provided by a fourth order Fresnel lens. The tower is now automated, and a 300mm acrylic lens produces the light source.

Scenic Route:

From Grand Haven return on Harbor to Columbus turn right. Go 0.9 miles to US-31 turn left. Go 0.9 miles to Ferrysburg exit. At ramp stop sign turn left on 3rd. (3rd jogs right and becomes 174th and then Grand Haven.) Go 3.8 miles to Pontaluna turn left. Pontaluna curves right and becomes Lake Harbor Drive. Go 6.5 miles to Seminole turn left. Go 0.3 miles to McCraken turn right. Go 1.2 miles to Sherman turn left. (Sherman becomes Beach St.) Go 2.6 miles to stop sign turn left. Go 0.9 miles to parking area near the Coast Guard building.

GPS Waypoints:

43° 225N
086° 4322W

Direct Route:

Take Business Rt. 31 / 96 from US-31 4.2 miles to Sherman turn left. Go 3.2 miles to Beach St. turn right. Go 1.9 miles to parking area. A second view from Muskegon State Park is available; see White River scenic for more details.

Attractions and Events

Museums:
> *Muskegon County Museum*
> > www.muskegonmuseum.org
>
> *Muskegon Museum of Art*
> > 231-722-2600
>
> *West Michigan Children's Museum*
>
> *USS Silversides & Maritime Museum*
> > www.silversides.org

Nature Center:
> *Gillette Nature Center*

Points of Interest:
> *Michigan Adventure Amusement Park*
> > www.miadventure.com
>
> *Hackley & Hume Historic Side*
> > 231-722-7578
>
> *Port City Princess*
> > 231-728-8387
>
> *Craig's Cruisers Family Fun Center*
> > 231-798-4836
>
> *World's Largest Weathervane*
> > 231-893-4585

Fairs & Festivals:
> **May**
> > **Spring Blooms**
> > 231-798-3711
>
> **June**
> > **Muskegon Summer Celebration**
>
> **July**
> > **Muskegon Air Fair**
> > www.muskegonairfair.com
>
> **August**
> > **Harbor Fest**
> > 800-250-WAVE
>
> **September**
> > **Michigan Irish Music Festival**
> > 800-250-WAVE
>
> **October**
> > **Muskegon County Convention & Visitors Bureau**
> > www.visitmuskegon.org
> > 800-250-WAVE

Contacts:

> **Muskegon County Convention & Visitors Bureau**
> > www.visitmuskegon.org
> > 800-250-WAVE
>
> **Muskegon Area Chamber of Commerce**
> > www.muskegon.org
> > 231-722-3751

7.) White River Lighthouse

It was no secret that Michigan's natural resources were untapped and plentiful. Almost any river that dumped into the Great Lakes had the potential to transport lumber to the lake. The White River was no exception. With the first saw mill built in this area in 1838, and subsequent ones to follow, the need for safe shipping was essential. Many ships were wrecked trying to enter the White River. In 1866, Congress allocated funds for channel improvement and lighthouse construction. When the construction ended in 1871, a light was positioned at the south pier's end. The power for this light was provided by a fifth order Fresnel lens. With an increase in shipping, it became apparent that a larger land-based lighthouse was needed. In 1875, White River had its first lighthouse. A fourth order Fresnel lens was installed in the lighthouse the following year. At this same time, the pier was extended and the pier light moved. Even with all the improvements, there still were an unusually high number of shipwrecks. In 1892, the light's characteristic was changed to improve visibility. Still unhappy with the results, the rotation speed of the light was increased in 1901. The fifth order lens in the pier head light was removed in 1902 and replaced with a sixth order lens. Later, in 1930, this light was replaced with the tower currently in use. The White River Lighthouse was deactivated in 1960. Within the lighthouse is a splendid museum that includes the original Fresnel lens.

Scenic Route:

From Pere Marquette Park turn right on Lakeshore, which changes to Laketon, go 4.2 miles turn left on Seaway, Business 31. Go 2.7 miles veer left on M-120 and follow the State Park sign. Go 1.4 miles turn left on Holton. Go 0.7 miles turn left on Ruddiman. Go 5.4 miles to stop sign. (Turn left here for additional view of Muskegon.) Turn right on Scenic Drive. Go 9.3 miles to stop sign turn left. Go 0.3 miles turn left on Murray. Go 1.1 miles to lighthouse parking. (Parking lot is small and cannot accommodate large RV's.)

GPS Waypoints:

43° 22.495N
086° 25.462W

Direct Route:

Exit US31 on White Lake Drive go west 4.5 miles. Turn left on South Shore. Go 3.5 miles to stop sign. Continue straight on Murray to lighthouse parking.

Attractions and Events

Museums:
> *White River Lightstation*
> > www.whiteriverlightstationorg
>
> *Muskegon County Museum*
> > 231-722-0278
>
> *Montague City Museum*

Points of Interest:
> *Michigan Adventure Amusement Park*
> > www.miadventure.com
>
> *World's Largest Weathervane*
> > 800-879-9702
>
> *Double J.J. Ranch*

Fairs & Festivals:
> **May**
> > **Spring Blooms**
> > 231-798-3711
>
> **June**
> > **Muskegon Summer Celebration**
> > www.summercelebration.com
> > **Annual Whitelake Area Arts & Crafts**
>
> **July**
> > **Blueberry Festival**
> > 231-766-3208
> > **Muskegon Air Fair**
> > www.muskegonairfair.com
> > **July 4th Festivities**
>
> **August**
> > **Harbor Fest**
> > 800-250-WAVE
> > **Maritime Festival**
> > 231-893-4585
>
> **September**
> > **Michigan Irish Music Festival**
> > 800-250-WAVE
> > **Octoberfest**
> > 231-893-4585
>
> **October**
> > **Muskegon Arts & Humanities Festival**
> > 231-777-0323
>
> **December**
> > **Annual Christmas Parade**

Contacts:
> **White Lake Area Chamber of Commerce**
> > www.whitelake.org
> > 231-893-4585

8.) Little Sable Point Light

The lumber movement that sprang up around the White River area also included the forests in this setting. Many ships that traveled north and south on Lake Michigan found themselves aground at Little Sable Point. The plea to Congress for a shoreline light at the point took full flight in 1871. The funding was approved, but this would prove to be no easy project. The problem was that there were no roads to this site. Eventually, work began in the spring of 1873. Even though construction was completed just prior to the winter of 1873, the light did not shine until the spring of 1874. Because of the color of the bricks, and the complaints from the ships about not being able to see the tower, it was painted white in 1900. The height of the tower is 107 feet tall and it houses a third order Fresnel lens. Electricity was routed to the lighthouse in 1954. The lighthouse was automated in 1955. That same year, the Coast Guard destroyed all the buildings, leaving only the tower. The tower remained white until 1977, when it was sand blasted and returned to its natural brick color. The tower is now a part of the Silver Lake State Park. Even though there is now easy access to this light, it still feels like it is out in the middle of nowhere.

Scenic Route:

Leave White River on Murray, then through the stop sign 3.5 miles. At stop sign turn left on South Shore go 1.1 miles to White Lake turn right. Go 1.1 miles turn left on Warner. Go 1.7 miles turn left on Colby. Go 1.1 miles turn right on Business 31. Go 5.6 miles to Webster turn left. (Business 31 ends at stop sign continue straight.) Go 6 miles Webster curves and becomes Scenic Drive. Go 10.3 miles turn right on Buchanan. Go 0.3 miles turn left on 18th Ave. Go 1.9 miles turn left on Silver Lake Rd. Go 0.5 miles turn right on 14th Ave. Go 1.2 miles to parking area.

GPS Waypoints:

44° 08.838N
086° 26.262W

Direct Route:

Exit US 31 at Shelby Rd go west 4.4 miles to Scenic Drive turn right. Go 1.3 miles to Buchanan turn right. Go 0.3 miles to 18th Ave turn left. Go 1.9 miles to Silver Lake Rd turn left. Go 0.5 miles to 14th Ave turn right. Go 1.2 miles to parking area.

Attractions and Events

Museums:
> *Oceana County Historical Society*
> 231-861-2965

Points of Interest:
> *Mac Wood's Dune Rides*
> www.macwoodsdunerides.com
> *Hart-Montague Bicycle Trail*
> *Sandy Korners Jeep Tours*
> www.sandykorners.com
> *Craig's Cruisers Fun Park*

Fairs & Festivals:
February
> **Annual Chocolate Fest**
> **Annual Snow Fest**

March
> **Annual St. Patrick's Day Parade**

April
> **Annual Easter Egg Hunt**

May
> **Mount Baldy Hill Climb**
> **Memorial Weekend Events**

June
> **National Asparagus Festival**
> **Annual Walkerville Pioneer Days**

July
> **July 4th Fireworks**
> **Annual Lakeshore Antique Garden Tractors Show**
> **Mears Art Fair**

August
> **Oceana County Fair**
> 231-873-2253
> **U.S. Sand Nationals**

September
> **Hart Heritage Days**
> **Shelby Apple Fest**

October
> **Halloween Parade**

November
> **Christmas Parade**

Contacts:

Shelby Area Chamber of Commerce
> 231-861-4054

Silver Lake Sand Dunes Area Chamber of Commerce
> www.silverlakesanddunes.com
> 231-873-5018

Hart-Silver Lake Area Chamber of Commerce
> www.oceana.com
> 231-873-2247

9.) Pentwater Pier Lights

Charles Mears was instrumental in the development of the harbor at Pentwater. In 1855, he built the channel that leads to Lake Michigan. The channel was necessary to allow ships to enter and access the sawmill he had built along the north shore. In 1867, a lighthouse, complete with a catwalk, was constructed on the south pier. In 1868, Congress approved funding for harbor improvements. The channel was made wider and deeper to allow larger ships to enter the harbor. With the increase of ship traffic, a life saving station was built on the north pier in 1887. The Coast Guard took over the operations of the lighthouse in 1915. The most notable shipwreck in the area occurred just off the shores of Pentwater in 1940. A dramatic storm with winds that ranged from 80 – 100 mph, and waves said to be 30 feet high, sank the *Anna C. Minch* and the *Wm. B. Davoc*, losing their entire crews. A third ship, the *Novadoc*, was also in peril from the waves. Local fisherman rallied together and saved all 17 of her crew. The lighthouse was destroyed in 1958. Automated towers on both north and south piers now guide mariners to the Pentwater Harbor.

Scenic Route:

From Little Sable return to the corner of Silver Lake and 18th Ave. Continue straight on Silver Lake Rd, it will jog right and become B15. Go 10.7 miles and B15 will jog right. Go 2.3 miles turn left on Business 31. Go 2.1 miles turn left on Lowell. Go 0.3 miles to parking area.

GPS Waypoints:

43° 46.946N
086° 26.625W

Direct Route:

From US 31 south of Pentwater exit Business Rt. 31 go north 3.1 miles to Lowell turn left. Go 0.3 miles to parking area.

From US 31 north of Pentwater exit Business Rt. 31 go south 3.5 miles to Lowell turn right. Go 0.3 miles to parking area.

Attractions and Events

Museums:
> *Oceana County Historical Society*
> 231-861-2965

Points of Interest:
> *A.J. Family Fun Center*
> 231-869-5641
> *Craig's Cruisers*
> 231-873-2511
> *Historic White Pine Village*
> www.historicwhitepinevillage.com

Fairs & Festivals:
April
> **Easter on the Green**
> **Annual English Tea**

May
> **Joe Pike Memorial Corvette Reunion**
> 231-869-5967
> **Annual Memorial Day Fishing Tournament**
> **Annual Memorial Day Parade**

June
> **Pentwater Spring Festival**
> 231-869-4150
> **Pickin in Pentwater**
> **National Asparagus Festival**
> **Annual Strawberry Shortcake Social**

July
> **Annual Pie Contest**
> **Annual Decorated Bicycle Parade**
> **Annual Powder Puff Mini Fishing Tournament**
> **Annual Fine Arts Fair**

August
> **Oceana County Fair**
> 231-873-2253
> **Annual Pentwater Homecoming Celebration**

September
> **Apple Fest**
> **Annual Fall Fest**

October
> **Annual Octoberfest**
> **Halloween On the Green**
> **Annual "One Sky, One World" Worldwide Kite Flying Event**
> 231-869-7004

December
> **Annual Christmas Craft Fair**

Contacts:
Pentwater Chamber of Commerce
> www.pentwater.com
> 800-870-9786

Oceana County Tourism Bureau
> 616-873-3928

10.) Ludington North Breakwater Light

Like so many other settlements along the Lake Michigan shore, the lumber industry dictated the growth of both population and maritime commerce. In 1867, funds were made available to the Army Corps of Engineers to improve the harbor and the river mouth entrance to Pere Marquette Lake. During these improvements, it was decided that a light on the pier was necessary. The light was situated at the end of the south pier in 1870. This 25 foot tall tower housed a fifth order Fresnel lens. Building the home for the keeper proved to be a little more difficult. Ultimately, the first keeper stayed in a shack at the base of the light. As it turned out, a terrible storm in 1876 destroyed the light and the keeper's shack. A new light was erected on the north pier in 1877. The south pier went through a series of extensions, and each time the light was moved to its end. After numerous attempts for funding, a fog signal building was finished in 1895. After 28 years, a keeper's home was finally built in 1900. Over the years it became a constant project of either extending or repairing the piers. In 1924, the current structure on the north breakwater was built. The tower is 57 feet tall, and at this time, housed a fourth order Fresnel lens. The south breakwater work was not completed until 1931. The North Breakwater light was automated in 1972. In 1994, while work was being done, the light settled. This left the light with the lean you can still see today.

Scenic Route:

From Pentwater return to Business 31 and turn left. Go 3.4 miles to Pere Marquette Hwy turn left. Go 10 miles to US 10 turn left. Go 2.4 miles to parking area.
(US 10 will end in town.)

GPS Waypoints:

43° 57.223N
086° 28.163W

Direct Route:

From US 31 and US 10 go west 3.8 miles to parking area.

Attractions and Events

Museums:
> *White Pine Village*
> > 231-843-4808
> *Rose Hawley Museum*
> > 231-843-2001

Points of Interest:
> *Lake Michigan Carferry Service*
> > www.ssbadgeer.com
> *Father Marquette Shrine*
> *Amber Elk Ranch*
> > 231-843-5ELK
> *Adventure Island Fun Park*
> > 231-843-3159
> *A.J. Family Fun Center*
> > 231-843-4838

Fairs & Festivals:
> **January**
> > **Lakeshore Ice Festival**
> > 800-542-4600
> **March**
> > **Annual Lake Jump**
> **June**
> > **Harbor Festival**
> > **Carferry Festival**
> **July**
> > **Western Michigan Fair**
> > 231-843-8563
> > **Fine Arts & Crafts Show**
> > 800-542-4600
> > **Freedom Festival**
> **August**
> > **Old Engine Show**
> > 800-542-4600
> > **Pioneer Logging Days**
> > 800-542-4600
> **September**
> > **Scottville Harvest Festival**
> > 800-542-4600
> **October**
> > **Octoberfest**
> > 800-542-4600

Contacts:
> **Ludington Chamber of Commerce**
> > www.ludginton.org
> > 231-845-0324
> **Ludington Area Convention & Visitors Bureau**
> > www.ludingtoncvb.com
> > 800-542-4600

11.) Big Sable Point Lighthouse

The members of the shipping industry felt it was necessary to have a light at Big Sable Point. Congress agreed; but first a dock had to be built because there were no roads to the site. In 1867, the 112 – foot tower was built. The source of light from this tower was provided by a third order Fresnel lens. The tower is constructed of brick. After the tower was built, the keeper's home was constructed. A problem surfaced with the brick tower when the brick began to fail. It was decided that the tower needed to be wrapped in steel. The work on the tower was finished in June of 1900. It was also at this time that the distinctive paint job on the tower was done. In 1909, the lighthouse was remodeled in order to incorporate a second keeper. Finally, in 1933, the first road reached the Big Sable Point Lighthouse. To protect the lighthouse from the wrath of Lake Michigan, a seawall was built around the tower in 1943. The modern marvel of electricity reached the light in 1949. Big Sable Point Lighthouse was automated in 1968, which meant that there was no need for a light keeper. The last keeper of Big Sable Point Lighthouse was Homer Meverden, who served from 1965 – 1968. The lighthouse is now part of the Ludington State Park.

Scenic Route:

From Ludington Beach parking area go east about one block turn left on M-116. Go 6.5 miles to State Park and parking area.

GPS Waypoints:

44° 03. 467N
086° 30.872W

Direct Route:

From the corner of US 10 and US 31 go west 3.7 miles to M-116 turn right. Go 6.5 miles to State Park and parking area.

Attractions and Events

Museums:
>*White Pine Village*
>>231-843-4808
>*Rose Hawley Museum*
>>231-843-2001

Points of Interest:
>*Lake Michigan Carferry Service*
>>www.ssbadgeer.com
>*Father Marquette Shrine*
>*Amber Elk Ranch*
>>231-843-5ELK
>*Adventure Island Fun Park*
>>231-843-3159
>*A.J. Family Fun Center*
>>231-843-4838

Fairs & Festivals:
>**January**
>>**Lakeshore Ice Festival**
>>800-542-4600
>**March**
>>**Annual Lake Jump**
>**May**
>>**Annual Wine & Cheese Event**
>>**Annual Ludington Poetry Festival**
>**June**
>>**Harbor Festival**
>>**Carferry Festival**
>**July**
>>**Western Michigan Fair**
>>231-843-8563
>>**Fine Arts & Crafts Show**
>>800-542-4600
>>**Freedom Festival**
>**August**
>>**Old Engine Show**
>>800-542-4600
>>**Pioneer Logging Days**
>>800-542-4600
>**September**
>>**Scottville Harvest Festival**
>>800-542-4600
>**October**
>>**Octoberfest**
>>800-542-4600
>**December**
>>**Annual Christmas Parade**

Contacts:
>**Ludington Chamber of Commerce**
>>www.ludginton.org
>>231-845-0324
>**Ludington Area Convention & Visitors Bureau**
>>www.ludingtoncvb.com
>>800-542-4600

12.) Manistee North Pierhead Light

Like so many other ports along the shores of Lake Michigan, the lumber industry was instrumental in the undertaking of harbor improvements and the establishment of a lighthouse at Manistee. A lighthouse was built along the shore in 1871. However, that light was destroyed in a fire later that year. With the completion of a 150 – foot addition to the piers, it was obvious that a shore light was not at all practical. So, in 1875, a light was installed on the end of the south pier. This light stood 27 feet tall and was powered by a fixed red fifth order lens. Once again, the pier was lengthened in 1879 and the light was moved seaward 156 feet. A fog signal was added to the south pier in 1890. Because of the large amount of ship traffic, it became necessary to reactivate the old shore lighthouse where the keepers were living. Now the keepers had three lights to maintain, including the chore of rowing out to the south pier. In 1894, the fog signal building was moved to the north pier, and the south pier lights were dismantled. In 1900, the fog signal building was moved to the pier's end. A breakwater pier was built along the south side of the river, and a light tower was raised in 1914. By 1925, the lights were run by electricity. Improvements on the piers continued, and in 1927, the fog signal building was dismantled. A steel tower standing 39 feet, and powered by a fifth order Fresnel lens, replaced the fog signal building. As is typical with many pier lights, Manistee Pierhead Light also had a catwalk to aid the keepers during rough seas.

Scenic Route:

From Big Sable parking area go south on M-116 to Lakeshore turn left. Go 0.2 miles turn right on Decker. Go 2 miles turn left on Jebavy. Go 2.2 miles turn right on Angling. Go 2.5 miles veer right on Fountain. Go 5.3 miles turn left on US 31. Go 15.1 miles turn left on Monroe, notice the Coast Guard sign. Go 0.7 miles and follow the sign to the beach. Veer right and go 0.4 miles to parking area.

GPS Waypoints:

44° 15.113N
086° 20.819

Direct Route:

From the corner of US 31 and M-55 go towards Manistee. Go 1.4 miles turn right on Monroe. Go 0.7 miles veer right. Go .4 miles to beach parking area.

Attractions and Events

Museums:
>*Manistee County Historical Museum*
>231-723-5531

Nature Center:
>*Lake Bluff Audubon Center*
>231-447-5511

Points of Interest:
>*Waterbug Tours*
>231-398-0919
>*City of Milwaukee Steamship*
>231-398-0328
>*The Trading Post*
>231-325-2202
>*Shomler Canoes, Kayaks and Rafts*
>231-862-3475

Fairs & Festivals:
March
>**Annual Regional High School Art Exhibit**
>www.westshore.edu

May
>**Annual Wheels of Steel Motorcycle Rodeo**

June
>**Spirit of the Woods Folk Festival**
>www.spiritofthewoods.org
>**Annual Flea Roast & Ox Market**
>www.ironsarea.com
>**Manistee National Forest Festival**
>800-288-2286

July
>**Bear Lake Days**

August
>**Manistee County Agricultural Fair**
>231-889-5566
>**Onekama Days**
>231-889-9650
>**Copemish Days**
>231-378-2616
>**Kaleva Heritage Days**
>www.kalevami.com

September
>**Port City Festival**
>231-723-2575

Contacts:
>**Manistee Area Chamber of Commerce**
>www.manistee.com
>800-288-2286
>**Manistee County Convention & Visitors Bureau**
>www.visitmanistee.com
>877-626-4783

13.) Frankfort North Breakwater Light

Had it not been for a nasty storm, the virtues of Lake Betsie may not have been discovered for many years. As luck would have it, however, a schooner ended up in the lake. Civilization soon followed. The townsfolk accomplished the first improvements to the harbor in 1859. As a result, the harbor soon became a popular spot of refuge. Plans were underway by 1867 to improve the harbor, complete with two piers that would allow ships to enter Lake Betsie. The work on the piers was completed in 1873. Shortly thereafter, construction began on the light, which was stationed on the north pier. The light source was provided by a red sixth order Fresnel lens. Construction on the piers to lengthen them began in 1884, and the south pier light was moved to the pier's end. In the fall of 1892, a fog bell building was built behind the pier light. Ship travel increased greatly in 1893, as railroad and car ferries traversed the Frankfort harbor. The decision was made to once again extend the piers. When completed in 1897, the light and fog signal building were moved. A second light was built to the rear of the pier to form range lights. A 44 – foot steel tower, with a red fourth order Fresnel lens, was built on the north pier in 1912. That same year, the lens from the south pier was repositioned behind the north pier, and the buildings on the south pier were destroyed. Electricity arrived to the lights at Frankfort in 1919. The breakwater piers that are seen today were finished in 1932. Upon completion, the north pierhead light was moved and placed on a base at the end of the breakwater, making its height 67 feet tall. By the mid 1960's, the ferries ceased to operate from Frankfort's harbor.

Scenic Route:

From Manistee return to US 31 turn left. Go 4.7 miles turn left on M-22. Go 29.1 miles turn left on Main. Go 1.1 miles to parking area.

GPS Waypoints:

44° 37.857N
086° 15.130W

Direct Route:

From M-115 heading west, turn left on 7th St. Go 1 block turn right on Main. Go 1 mile to parking area.

Attractions and Events

Museums:

> *Benzie Area Historical Museum*
> 231-882-5539

Points of Interest:

> *Father Marquette Cross &*
> *Historical Marker*
>
> *Mineral Springs Park*
>
> *Fun Country Family Fun Center*
> 231-276-6360

Fairs & Festivals:
February
> **Winterfest**

June
> **Spring Craft Fair**
> 231-352-7251
> **Northwood Renaissance Festival**
> 231-885-1185

July
> **July 4th Celebration**
> **Annual Art & Craft**
> 231-352-7251
> **Beulah Art Fair**
> 231-325-6642
> **Annual Honor Car Show**
> 231-882-4063

August
> **Annual Collector Car Show**
> **Benzie Fishing Frenzy**
> 231-352-7251
> **Annual Frankfort Airshow**
> 231-352-7251
> **Blueberry Festival**
> 231-352-7251

October
> **Great Pumpkin Day**

November
> **Annual Holly Berry Arts &**
> **Crafts Fair**
> 231-352-7251

Contacts:

> **Benzie County Chamber of Commerce**
> www.benzie.com
> 800-882-5801
>
> **Frankfort-Elberta Area Chamber**
> **of Commerce**
> www.frankfort-elberta.com
> 231-352-7251

14.) Point Betsie Lighthouse

While a lighthouse on South Manitou Island helped mark the infamous Manitou Passage, it eventually became clear that a light was needed on the mainland to assist mariners plotting their course through the passage. Funds for the lighthouse were approved in 1853, but construction was not completed until 1858. Point Betsie's tower is 37 feet tall and was equipped with a white fourth order Fresnel lens. In 1869, it became necessary to reinforce the sand dunes at the base of the lighthouse. Waves crashing to shore loosened not only the sand, but some of the light's foundation as well. Six years later, a life saving station was built to the south of the lighthouse. In 1880, plans were made to renovate the light, including changing the tower height to 100 feet. Those changes were never made because funding was not approved. Through 1889, and 1890, the foundation of the tower, and the seawall were reinforced. Just north of the lighthouse a fog signal building was built in 1891. Because of the additional workload, the lighthouse's first assistant keeper was hired in 1892. Workers arrived at the lighthouse in 1895 to renovate the keeper's dwelling so that it could accommodate two families. Point Betsie was given its familiar white paint and red roof in 1900. Electricity arrived at the lighthouse in 1921. The original fourth order lens was removed in 1996. Point Betsie Lighthouse was the last Lake Michigan lighthouse to be automated. This occurred in 1984.

Scenic Route:

From Frankfort parking area go back on Main 1 mile turn left on 7th. Go 1 block. Continue straight, this is now M-22. Go 4.2 miles turn left on Point Betsie Rd. Go 0.7 miles to lighthouse.

GPS Waypoints:

44° 41.471N
086° 15.311W

Direct Route:

From the corner of M-115 and M-22 turn north. Go 4.2 miles turn left on Point Betsie Rd. Go 0.7 miles to lighthouse.

Attractions and Events

Museums:

Benzie Area Historical Museum
231-882-5539

Points of Interest:

*Father Marquette Cross &
Historical Marker*

Mineral Springs Park

Fun Country Family Fun Center
231-276-6360

Fairs & Festivals:
February
Winterfest
June
Spring Craft Fair
231-352-7251
Northwood Renaissance Festival
231-885-1185
July
July 4th Celebration
Annual Art & Craft
231-352-7251
Beulah Art Fair
231-325-6642
Annual Honor Car Show
231-882-4063
August
Annual Collector Car Show
Benzie Fishing Frenzy
231-352-7251
Annual Frankfort Airshow
231-352-7251
Blueberry Festival
231-352-7251
October
Great Pumpkin Day
November
**Annual Holly Berry Arts &
Crafts Fair**
231-352-7251

Contacts:

Benzie County Chamber of Commerce
www.benzie.com
800-882-5801

**Frankfort-Elberta Area Chamber
of Commerce**
www.frankfort-elberta.com
231-352-7251

15.) Robert H. Manning Memorial Light

The Robert H. Manning Memorial Light is currently one of three memorial lights in Michigan. The two others are the William Livingstone Memorial Light and the Mariners Memorial Light. Robert Manning was a life-long resident of the Empire area. Fishing was an integral part of his life, so naturally he spent many days in his boat out on Lake Michigan. He often told those that would listen that a lighthouse here would make his return trips easier. Robert H. Manning died in 1989 at the age of 62. Mr. Manning's family set out to build a light in Empire to honor his memory. With the monetary help from those that knew him, the Robert H. Manning Memorial Light was built in 1990. The light is located in the Empire Beach Park. If you plan to photograph this light, we recommend you arrive either early in the day or towards sunset. The park is not large and it is very busy in the summer.

Scenic Route:

From Point Betsie return to M-22 turn left. Go 18.3 miles turn left on Front St. Go 0.3 miles turn right on Lake. Go 1 block turn left on Niagra. Go 0.2 miles to park entrance. (If you are going to photograph this light, we suggest early in the day or at sunset. This is a very busy park in the summer.)

GPS Waypoints:

44° 48.843N
086° 04.034W

Direct Route:

From Traverse City take M-72 west. M-72 ends at Front St. Go 0.3 miles turn right on Lake. Go 1 block turn left on Niagra. Go 0.2 miles to park entrance.

Attractions and Events

Museums:
> *Empire Area Heritage Museum*
> 231-326-5566
> *Sleeping Bear Point Maritime Museum*
> 231-326-5134
> *Leelanau Historical Society & Museum*
> 231-256-7475

Nature Center:
> *Sleeping Bear Dunes Visitors Center*
> 231-326-5134

Points of Interest:
> *Riverside Canoe Trips*
> www.canoemichigan.com
> *Sleeping Bear Dunes*

Fairs & Festivals:
> **May**
> > **Annual Hatties Michigan Art Exhibition**
> **June**
> > **Leeland Wine & Food Festival**
> **July**
> > **Empire Anchor Days**
> > **Suttons Bay Annual Zazzfest**
> > 231-271-4444
> **August**
> > **Northport Red, White & the Blues Wine & Food Festival**
> > 231-271-9895
> > **Annual Wodsley Airport Fly In**
> > **Dune Grass Festival**
> **October**
> > **Fiber Festival**
> > 231-256-2131

Contacts:
> **Leelanau Peninsula Chamber of Commerce**
> > www.leelanauchamber.com
> > 800-980-9895
> **Glenlake/Sleeping Bear Chamber of Commerce**
> > www.leelanau.com/glenlake
> > 231-333-3238

16.) South Manitou Island Lighthouse

South Manitou Island is the southern most point of the Manitou Passage. By using this passage, ships cut delivery time by decreasing mileage. The harbor at Manitou Island was a common spot for ships to wait out storms on Lake Michigan. There was no debating the need for a light marking the southern entrance to the passage, so in 1839 construction began. The quality of material and workmanship on the original light apparently were less than stellar. The first light stood 1.5 stories. The building was made of stone, and the light tower sat atop the roof on the lakeside. After numerous complaints about the light's effectiveness, and the forming of the Lighthouse Board, the lanterns in the tower were replaced with a fourth order Fresnel lens in 1857. While installing the new lens, workers discovered numerous unsafe conditions within the lighthouse. That next year, 1858, workers built a brand new lighthouse and the lens was relocated into the new tower atop the roof. While they were on the island, and to aid navigation in bad weather, a fog bell building and bell were installed. As before, illumination from the South Manitou Light was not satisfactory. As a result, construction on a much larger tower and lens began in 1871. When construction concluded in 1872, the new South Manitou Light had a tower standing 91 feet and was equipped with a third order Fresnel lens. A new fog signal building that featured a locomotive whistle fueled by steam was built in 1875. Three years later, a second equally equipped fog signal building was built. The year 1893 saw the conversion from lamp oil to kerosene, and the construction of the necessary storage building. The fog signals were updated in 1933. As technology advanced, and the North Manitou Shoal Light was built, the usefulness of South Manitou Island Lighthouse waned. Finally in 1958, this 118 - year old light was deactivated.

GPS Waypoints:

45° 008N
086° 0943W

Direct Route:

Manitou Island Transit
www.leelanua.com/manitou/manitou.html
231-256-9061

Attractions and Events

Contacts:

Sleeping Bear Dunes National Lakeshore
www.nps.gov/slbe
231-326-4134

Glen Lake/Sleeping Bear Chamber of Commerce
www.leelanau.com/glenlake
231-333-3238

Leelanau Peninsula Chamber of Commerce
www.leelanauchamber.com
231-256-9895

Manitou Island Transit
www.leelanau.com/manitou
231-256-9061

17.) North Manitou Shoal Light

Like many of the offshore shoals and reefs in Lake Michigan, a lightship first marked North Manitou Shoal. The shoal is located between Manitou Island and Pyramid Point. Mariners felt a light was necessary to mark the shoals, thereby ensuring safe navigation of the Manitou Passage. There were three lightships that marked the shoals. They were lightships LV89, LV103, and WAL526. These lightships served at different intervals beginning in 1910. Like most offshore lights, the timber crib foundation was completed on the mainland and then towed to its location. Once at the selected location, the crib would be lowered into the water and construction would begin. Much of the North Manitou Shoal Light's work was done in Frankfort. When the light was completed in 1935, the lightship was no longer needed. The tower of the North Manitou Shoal Light stands 63 feet and originally used a fourth order Fresnel lens. The lighthouse is comprised of the crib, a five story building which includes: a) the maintenance area for the lighthouse b) living areas c) and three areas used for observation. Forty-five years after conception, North Manitou Shoal Light was automated, making it the last light in the Great Lakes to have a manned crew. Solar power was incorporated at the light in 2000.

GPS Waypoints:

45° 0199N
085° 9563W

Direct Route:

Manitou Island Transit
www.leelanua.com/manitou/manitou.html
231-256-9061

Attractions and Events

Contacts:

Sleeping Bear Dunes National Lakeshore
www.nps.gov/slbe
231-326-4134

Glen Lake/Sleeping Bear Chamber of Commerce
www.leelanau.com/glenlake
231-333-3238

Leelanau Peninsula Chamber of Commerce
www.leelanauchamber.com
231-256-9895

Manitou Island Transit
www.leelanau.com/manitou
231-256-9061

Lighthouse Journal

Lighthouse	Date Visited	Comments
1.		
2.		
3.		
4.		
5.		
6.		
7.		
8.		
9.		
10.		
11.		
12.		
13.		
14.		
15.		
16.		

Squaw Island Lighthouse

White Shoal Light

Little Sable Point

Ludington North Pier Light

Beaver Harbor

South Haven Pier Light

Lansing Shoal Light

Gray's Reef Light

Grand Haven Pier Lights

Point Betsie Lighthouse

White River Lighthouse

Holland Harbor Light

Manistee North Pier Light

St. Joeseph Pier Lights

South Manitou Island Lighthouse

Charlevoix South Pier Light

Waugoshance Shoal Light

Grand Traverse Lighthouse

Frankfort Breakwater Light

Big Sable Point

Skillagalee Island Light

Lighthouse Journal

Lighthouse	Date Visited	Comments
17.		
18.		
19.		
20.		
21.		
22.		
23.		
24.		
25.		
26.		
27.		
28.		
29.		
30.		
31.		
32.		

18.) Grand Traverse Lighthouse

The Grand Traverse Lighthouse is built on what is called Cat's Head Point. It is at the point that ships would make their turn to the Straits of Mackinac or into Grand Traverse Bay. With this important fact in mind, it was deemed necessary to build a lighthouse, which was established in 1852. The first light keeper at Grand Traverse was David Moon. After only five years, it was determined that the foundation of the lighthouse was in peril. In 1858, the original lighthouse was torn down. A new lighthouse, complete with a white fifth order Fresnel lens was built. In 1869, the lens was changed to a fourth order lens. With the increase in shipping traffic, and the notorious weather conditions, it was decided that Grand Traverse needed to be equipped with a fog signal. The necessary funds were allocated and the finished fog signal began its service to navigation in 1899. Since the workload at the light had increased, an assistant keeper was needed. The first assistant at the light was hired in 1901, after modifications were made to the keeper's home to accommodate a second family. In 1933, the whistles and boilers were removed from the fog signal building. The Coast Guard maintained the light at Grand Traverse until an automated steel tower was installed in 1972. The Grand Traverse Lighthouse is now a part of Leelanau State Park. Today the lighthouse is a museum operated by the Grand Traverse Lighthouse Foundation. The museum was first opened to the public in 1987.

Scenic Route:

From Robert Manning return to M-22 turn left. Go 37.8 miles of numerous twists and turns to stop sign in Northport. Turn left on M-201 go 0.4 miles turn right. Go 1 block turn left. Go 1.1 miles M-201 becomes CR640. Go 1.5 miles CR640 becomes CR629. Go 5.7 miles to the State Park.

GPS Waypoints:

45° 12.612N
085° 32.990W

Direct Route:

From Traverse City at the corner of M-72 and M-22 take M-22 north 27 miles. M-22 becomes M-201 go 0.4 miles turn right. Go 1 block turn left. Go 1.1 miles M-201 becomes CR640. Go 1.5 miles CR640 becomes CR629. Go 5.7 miles to the State Park.

Attractions and Events

Museums:
> *Leelanau Historical Museum*
>> 231-256-7475
> *This Ole Farm Museum*
>> 231-269-3672
> *Grand Traverse Heritage Center*
>> 231-995-0313
> *Sleeping Bear Point Maritime Museum*
>> 231-326-5134

Points of Interest:
> *Clinch Park Zoo*
> *Tall Ship Sailing Adventure*
>> www.tallshipsailing.com
> *Pirate's Cove Adventure Park*
>> 231-938-9599
> *Grand Traverse Balloon Rides*
>> 231-947-7433
> *Ranch Rudolf*
>> 231-947-9529

Fairs & Festivals:
January
> Kalkaska Winterfest/Sled Dog Races

May
> Mancelona Bass Festival

June
> Northwood Renaissance Festival
> 231-885-1540

July
> National Cherry Festival
> www.cherryfestival.org
> Traverse Bay Outdoor Artfair
> 231-941-9488
> Suttons Bay Jazz fest
> 231-271-4444
> Grand Traverse Lighthouse
> Celebration
> 231-386-7195

August
> Northwestern Michigan Fair
> Classic Boats on the Boardwalk
> 269-372-3321
> Suttons Bay Community Art Festival
> Annual Rubber Ducky Festival
> Annual Buckley Old Engine Show
> Classic Car Show

September
> Classic Boat Show
> Model Train Show

October
> Alden Halloween Celebration
> Alden Vintage Car Show

November
> Annual Christmas Art & Craft
> Show
> 231-941-9488

Contacts:
Traverse City Convention &
Visitor Bureau
> www.tcvisitor.com
> 800-872-8377

Traverse City Chamber of Commerce
> www.tcchamber.com
> 800-872-8377

Leelanau Peninsula Chamber of Commerce
> www.leelanauchamber.com
> 800-980-9895

19.) Old Mission Point Lighthouse

Mission Point got its name based on a treaty with the Ottawa Indians. The government was to provide a mission and schools for the reservation. This area is known for its fertile soil and bountiful harvest. Ships traveled into both east and west bays to transport produce to waiting customers. Shoals stretch out from the peninsula into the bays, so it was obvious that a navigational aid was needed. Funding for a light was approved in 1859, however, the Civil War interfered with those plans. Construction was finally completed on the Mission Point Lighthouse in 1870. The lighthouse features a 36 – foot tower and a white fifth order Fresnel lens. In those days, high water levels were common. In fact, in 1889 a wooden sea wall was built along the shore to help stem problems with erosion. The fence around the lighthouse was installed in 1901, as sightseers were a problem even in those days. In 1933, a steel skeletal tower was built on shore and the lighthouse was deactivated. With the advancements in technology, it was decided that the shoals would be marked more efficiently at their points of origin. In 1938, work began on what was basically a crib at the site of the shoals. When it was finished, a 36 – foot tall steel tower flashed a white light identifying the area of the shoals. Some years later, the current cylindrical D-9 tower replaced the original steel tower. The grounds at Old Mission Point are open, but the park's manager occupies the lighthouse.

Scenic Route:

From Grand Traverse return to the corner of M-201 and M-22. Take M-22 south 29.6 miles to M-37 turn left. (M-22 will merge with M-72/M-37 in Traverse City.) Go 18.2 miles to Lighthouse Park.

GPS Waypoints:

44° 59.471N
085° 28.787W

Direct Route:

In Traverse City at the corner of M-72/US31 turn north on M-37. Go 18.2 miles to Lighthouse Park.

Attractions and Events

Museums:
> *Music House Museum*
> > 231-938-9300
> *This Ole Farm Museum*
> > 231-269-3672
> *Dennos Museum Center*
> > 231-995-1055
> *Grand Traverse Heritage Center*
> > 231-995-0313

Points of Interest:
> *Clinch Park Zoo*
> *Tall Ship Sailing Adventure*
> > www.tallshipsailing.com
> *Pirate's Cove Adventure Park*
> > 231-938-9599
> *Grand Traverse Balloon Rides*
> > 231-947-7433
> *Ranch Rudolf*
> > 231-947-9529

Fairs & Festivals:
January
> **Kalkaska Winterfest/Sled Dog Races**
May
> **Mancelona Bass Festival**
June
> **Northwood Renaissance Festival**
> 231-885-1540
July
> **National Cherry Festival**
> www.cherryfestival.org
> **Traverse Bay Outdoor Art Fair**
> 231-941-9488
> **Suttons Bay Jazz fest**
> 231-271-4444
> **Grand Traverse Lighthouse**
> **Celebration**
> 231-386-7195
August
> **Northwestern Michigan Fair**
> **Classic Boats on the Boardwalk**
> 269-372-3321
> **Suttons Bay Community Art Festival**
> 231-271-5077
> **Annual Rubber Ducky Festival**
> **Annual Buckley Old Engine Show**
> **Classic Car Show**
September
> **Classic Boat Show**
> **Model Train Show**
October
> **Alden Halloween Celebration**
> **Alden Vintage Car Show**
November
> **Annual Christmas Art & Craft Show**
> 231-941-9488

Contacts:
Traverse City Convention & Visitor Bureau
> www.tcvisitor.com
> 800-872-8377
Traverse City Chamber of Commerce
> www.tcchamber.com
> 800-872-8377

20.) Charlevoix South Pier Light

Most settlements along the shores of Lake Michigan were established as a result of the lumber industry, and Charlevoix was no exception. For years, ships moored to a dock situated on the Pine River to receive the lumber. This proved to be a less than perfect remedy because of its need for constant repairs. At first the locals dug the channel by hand and sunk cribs to form a pier. In 1884, a light was placed on the north pier to aid navigation. The 30 – foot tower housed a fifth order Fresnel lens. A life saving station was built on the north shore in 1900. Also that same year, modifications were made to the north pier by raising the light. When the work was completed, the light was lowered back down to the pier. A fog bell was erected on the pier, ready to work in 1909. Extensive renovations were made to both the north and south piers in 1914. When the work was finished, the light was moved from the north to the south pier and painted red. On the north pier, a 56 – foot tall steel tower was raised at its end. When electricity was introduced in 1938, the old fog bell was upgraded and the lamp in the pier light was converted as well. The decision was made in 1947 to replace the original wood constructed light on the south pier, with a new steel-built light. The life saving station at Charlevoix was moved in 1965. The last change to the Charlevoix South Pier Light occurred around 1980 when it was painted white.

Scenic Route:

Return to the intersection of M-37 and M-72 / US31 turn left. Go 49 miles on US31 to Park St. turn left. Go 0.4 miles to Grant turn right. Parking area is one block ahead.

GPS Waypoints:

45° 19.216N
085° 15.899W

Direct Route:

From US31 in Charlevoix go west 0.4 miles on Park St. Park St. is one block south of the bridge. Turn right on Grant. Parking area is one block ahead.

Attractions and Events

Museums:
> *Raven Hill Discovery Center*
> 231-536-3369
> *Harsha House Museum*
> 231-547-0373
> *Railroad Depot Museum*
> www.chxhistory.com

Points of Interest:
> *Ironton Ferry*
> *Beaver Island Boat Company*
> www.bibc.com
> *Cedar Valley Farms*
> 231-547-7352

Fairs & Festivals:
April
> **Annual Easter Egg Hunt**

May
> **Memorial Day Parade**
> **Boyne City Mushroom Festival**

June
> **Jordon Valley Freedom Festival**
> 231-536-7351
> **Lake Charlevoix Trout Tournament**

July
> **Charlevoix Downtown Art Festival**
> www.artfestival. com
> **Charlevoix Chamber's Art's & Craft Show**
> 231-547-2101
> **Charlevoix Venetian Festival**
> www.ventianfestival.com
> **Polish Festival**
> 231-582-6222
> **Car Show**
> 231-536-7351

August
> **Charlevoix Waterfront Art Fair**
> 231-547-2675
> **Street Legends Car Show**
> **Annual Portside Art Fair**
> 231-536-7351

September
> **Red Fox Regata**

October
> **Charlevoix Apple Festival**
> **Boyne City Fall Harvest Festival**
> 231-582-6222

Contacts:
Charlevoix Area Chamber of Commerce
> www.charlevoix.com
> 231-547-2101

Boyne City Chamber of Commerce
> www.boynecity.com
> 231-582-6222

East Jordan Chamber of Commerce
> www.eastjordonchamberofcommerce.com
> 231-536-7351

21.) Petoskey Pier Light

There is very little published historical information concerning the Petoskey Pier Light. The majority of ship traffic entered the area headed for Little Traverse. Petoskey needed a light however to guide ships entering its harbor. The original light in Petoskey was established in 1899. That light was a pagoda-style structure. The Petoskey Light is cylindrical, and constructed of concrete and steel. Originally, the entire light was painted red. Today, the current tower's concrete base is red and the steel tower is white. Sometime between 1910 and 1930 the light was destroyed and eventually replaced by the current light. The Petoskey light is typical of most pierhead lights sitting at the end of a break wall. The light helps guide present day vessels into the Petoskey Marina.

Scenic Route:

From Charlevoix return to US31 and turn left. Go 16.8 miles turn left on Lake St. at the stop light. Go 2 blocks to marina and museum parking area. Additional parking is available 3 blocks south by turning right on Wachtel.

GPS Waypoints:

45° 22.807N
084° 57.694W

Direct Route:

From the corner of US31 and Lake St. in Petoskey turn south on Lake St. Go 2 blocks to marina and museum parking area. Additional parking is available 3 blocks south by turning right on Wachtel.

Attractions and Events

Museums:
> *Ravenhill Discovery Center*
> 877-833-4254
> *Little Traverse History Museum*
> 231-347-2620
> *Crooked Tree Arts Center*
> 231-347-4337
> *Bay Harbor History Museum*
> 231-347-2620

Nature Center:
> *Little Traverse Conservancy*
> 231-347-0991

Points of Interest:
> *Northern Michigan Hardwoods*
> 231-347-4575
> *Romanik's Ranch*
> 231-347-6106
> *Stoney Lane Farm*
> 231-539-8186

Fairs & Festivals:
January
> **Annual Bay Harbor Ice Festival**

February
> **Winter Carnival**
> **Annual Bay Harbor Mush**

May
> **National Morel Mushroom Festival**

June
> **Annual Gallery Walk**
> **Jordan Valley Freedom Festival**
> **Wolverine Lumberjack Festival**

July
> **Annual Juried Fine Arts Exhibition**
> **Fireworks Celebration**
> **Annual Blissfest**
> **Annual Custom Car Show**

August
> **Annual Bay Harbor Summer Arts Fair**
> **Festival on the Bay**
> **Emmet County Fair**

September
> **Annual Mopars By the Bay**

October
> **Harvest Festival**

November
> **Holiday Parade**
> **Annual Festival of Trees**

Contacts:

Petoskey Regional Chamber of Commerce
> www.petoskey.com
> 231-347-4150

Boyne County Convention & Visitors Bureau
> www.boynecountry.com
> 800-845-2822

22.) Little Traverse Bay Lighthouse

Even though the Harbor Springs area was home to a large population of Ottawa Indians, the lumber companies moved into the area around 1853. By the year 1855, a request for Federal monies for harbor improvements and a lighthouse were made. The first attempt was denied. Both the population and commercialization of the area began to skyrocket. A second request was made for funding in 1882; this time it was successful. Finally, in 1884, the Little Traverse Lighthouse, with a 30 – foot tower and a red fourth order Fresnel lens, began its service. Harbor Springs was fast becoming a vacation and summer home destination. As a result, in order to aid navigation, a fog bell tower was positioned on the point in front of the lighthouse in 1896. Life was very peaceful at Little Traverse. The largest change to occur at Little Traverse was a switch from sperm oil to kerosene as the source of fuel for the light. As a result, an oil storage building was built to reduce the risk of fire in the dwelling. Control of the lighthouse was given to the Coast Guard in 1939. The final changed to arrive at the lighthouse occurred in 1963. A 41 – foot tall steel tower was built as automation arrived. The fog bell tower, as well as the fourth order Fresnel lens, is still intact at the lighthouse.

Directions:

Little Traverse Lighthouse is located within a private gated community with no public access.

GPS Waypoints:

45° 4188N
084° 9782W

Attractions and Events

Museums:
- *Ravenhill Discovery Center*
  877-833-4254
- *Little Traverse History Museum*
  231-347-2620
- *Bay Harbor History Museum*
  231-347-2620

Nature Center:
- *Little Traverse Conservancy*
  231-347-0991

Points of Interest:
- *Romanik's Ranch*
  231-347-6106
- *Bayer Glassworks*
  231-526-6359
- *Morjan Trout Farm*
  231-548-4114
- *Oden State Fish Hatchery*
  231-347-4689

Fairs & Festivals:

January
- **Annual Bay Harbor Ice Festival**

February
- **Winter Carnival**

May
- **National Morel Mushroom Festival**

June
- **Jordan Valley Freedom Festival**
- **Wolverine Lumberjack Festival**

July
- **Alpenfest**
- **Harbor Springs Women's Club Art Fest**
- **Annual Shay Days**
- **Venetian Festival**
- **Flywheelers Engine & Craft Show**

August
- **Polish Festival**
- **Bay Harbor Summer Art Fair**

October
- **Fall Harvest Festival**
  231-582-6222
- **Harbor Springs Fall Festival**
  231-526-7999
- **Annual Leaf Peekers Craft Show**

Contacts:

Petoskey Regional Chamber of Commerce
www.petoskey.com
231-347-4150

Harbor Springs Chamber of Commerce
www.harborspringschamber.com
231-526-7999

Boyne County Convention & Visitors Bureau
www.boynecountry.com
800-845-2822

23.) South Fox Island Lighthouse

South Fox Island is nestled in Lake Michigan between North Manitou Island and Beaver Island. In 1867, Congress approved the necessary funds, and the wheels were set in motion to build a lighthouse on Fox Island. Construction on the light began that spring, and by November the light was seen for the first time. Inside the tower, a flashing red fourth order Fresnel lens guided the ships that passed nearby. The original foghorn on the island was fueled by steam. Later, the fog warning system would be upgraded to the typical diaphone fog signal. At some point, a switch was made from lard oil to kerosene as the light's fuel source. So as to not subject the lighthouse to the highly flammable liquid, an oil storage building was constructed in 1892. Near the lighthouse, an assistant keeper's quarters were built in 1898. The year 1910 saw construction of a red brick assistant keeper's dwelling that would replace the original wooden structure. Maintenance at the lighthouse was never-ending. As a result, it was decided to replace the 1867 lighthouse with a steel tower from Sapelo Island, Georgia. In 1933, the tower was dismantled and shipped to South Fox Island. In 1934, workers gathered at South Fox Island to reassemble the tower. Unfortunately, due to conflicting information, it is not exactly known when the island was abandoned.

Directions:

South Fox Island is located in Lake Michigan and can be seen by boat or plane only. The South Fox Island Restoration Project, www.southfoxisland.us.tc are planning tours in the future. Contact them for more details. We took Island Hopper Charters, www.islandhopper.beaverisland.net.

GPS Waypoints:

45° 3798N
085° 8361W

Attractions and Events

Contacts:

Beaver Island Boat Company
    www.bibc.com

Island Airways
    www.islandairways.com

Island Hopper Charters
    www.islandhopper.beaverisland.net

Beaver Island Chamber of Commerce
    www.beaverisland.org

Charlevoix Area Chamber of Commerce
    www.charlevoix.org

24.) Beaver Island Harbor Light

Once a strong Irish fishing community, life on Beaver Island changed dramatically with the rule of James Strang and his band of Mormons. The stranglehold Strang had on the island dissipated when he was shot in 1856. That same year, the Beaver Island Harbor Light was built. However, this facility was crude at best. The first light keeper at Whiskey Point was Lyman Granger. As shipping increased in the frequency and number of vessels, Congress was asked to approve funding for a larger and more efficient light. In 1867, the funding was approved. A new 1.5 story brick lighthouse with a 41 – foot tall tower was built. Inside the tower, a fourth order Fresnel lens was positioned for service. Tragedy struck the light keepers in 1872. While trying to rescue any survivors of a sinking boat, Clement Van Riper and the first mate of the schooner *Thomas Howland*, disappeared into the night, never to be seen again. Clement's wife Elizabeth was named keeper of the light after the loss. In 1855, remodeling and restoration took place at the light. Included in the construction was a building to store kerosene, which was to become the fuel source for the light. Automation reached the Beaver Harbor Lighthouse, also known as St. James Harbor Light, in 1927. With automation complete, the Coast Guard kept watch on the light from the lifesaving post nearby. Since no keeper was now required, all of the buildings were leveled, leaving only the tower. The tower is still an important tool in today's navigation.

Directions:

Beaver Island is located in Lake Michigan and can be reached by boat or plane. We took Beaver Island Boat Company out of Charlevoix. The web site is www.bibco.com.

GPS Waypoints:

45° 7425N
085° 5088W

Attractions and Events

Museums:
> *Mormon Print Shop*
>
> *Maritime Museum*
>
> *Toy Museum*

Nature Center:
> *C.M.U. Biological Station*
> 231-448-2325

Points of Interest:
> *Inland Seas School of Kayaking*
> 231-448-2221
> *Unfinished Farms Riding Stable*
> 231-448-2639
> *Emerald Isles Gallery*
> 231-448-2844
> *Seven Sisters*
> 231-448-2060

Fairs & Festivals:
> **March**
>> St. Patrick's Day Celebration
>
> **July**
>> 4th of July Parade & Fireworks
>> Museum Week
>> Charlevoix Venetian Festival
>> Boyne City Polish Festival
>
> **August**
>> Beaver Island Homecoming
>> Celebration
>
> **October**
>> Charlevoix Apple Festival
>> Boyne City Fall Harvest Festival
>> 231-582-6222

Contacts:

> **Beaver Island Chamber of Commerce**
>> www.beaverisland.com
>> 231-448-2505
>
> **Charlevoix Area Chamber of Commerce**
>> www.charlevoix.com
>> 231-547-2101
>
> **Boyne City Chamber of Commerce**
>> www.boynecity.com
>> 231-582-6222

25.) Beaver Head Light

As early as 1830, ship captains began requesting that a light be placed at the south end of Beaver Island. Some representatives agreed, and asked for funding in 1838. Finally, in 1850, Congress granted the request. As it turns out, the proposed location for the lighthouse was on land that the Federal Government owned. That fact accelerated the process, and in 1851, Beaver Head Lighthouse was established. Unfortunately, the materials and the craftsmanship were less than perfect. So, in 1858, the lighthouse was overhauled and the 46 – foot tower became equipped with a fourth order Fresnel lens. Ice flows damaged the boat landing and required repair in 1886. Again the next winter, ice was a problem as it destroyed the boathouse. In 1890, Skillagalee received a new fog whistle and its fog siren was sent to Beaver Head. The fog signal building was built along with a rail system to transport coal from the docks to the buildings. With these additional improvements, the workload was more than two keepers could handle. So, in 1902, an addition was added to the keeper's home to accommodate a third keeper. Over the next several years, improvements and renovations were made. 1906 saw the rail system extended and cement sidewalks constructed. In 1915, the fog signal was upgraded. In 1938, electricity arrived at Beaver Head Lighthouse, which in turn led to a modification of the beacon. The Coast Guard took control of the operation of the light in 1939. It wasn't until 1953 that the lighthouse had a telephone. Finally in 1962, Beaver Head Lighthouse was deactivated.

Directions:

Beaver Island is located in Lake Michigan and can be reached by boat or plane. We took Beaver Island Boat Company out of Charlevoix. The web site is www.bibco.com.

GPS Waypoints:

45° 5773N
085° 5763W

Attractions and Events

Museums:
> *Mormon Print Shop*
> *Maritime Museum*
> *Toy Museum*

Nature Center:
> *C.M.U. Biological Station*
> 231-448-2325

Points of Interest:
> *Inland Seas School of Kayaking*
> 231-448-2221
> *Unfinished Farms Riding Stable*
> 231-448-2639
> *Emerald Isles Gallery*
> 231-448-2844
> *Seven Sisters*
> 231-448-2060

Fairs & Festivals:
March
> **St. Patrick's Day Celebration**

July
> **4th of July Parade & Fireworks**
> **Museum Week**
> **Charlevoix Venetian Festival**
> **Boyne City Polish Festival**

August
> **Beaver Island Homecoming Celebration**

October
> **Charlevoix Apple Festival**
> **Boyne City Fall Harvest Festival**
> 231-582-6222

Contacts:
> **Beaver Island Chamber of Commerce**
> www.beaverisland.com
> 231-448-2505
> **Charlevoix Area Chamber of Commerce**
> www.charlevoix.com
> 231-547-2101
> **Boyne City Chamber of Commerce**
> www.boynecity.com
> 231-582-6222

26.) Squaw Island Lighthouse

The waters around Squaw Island were extremely shallow. In some places the water was only six feet deep. This fact was a deciding factor for the placement of a light on Squaw Island. In 1891, Congress approved funding for the construction of the lighthouse to warn vessels of the danger. Construction began in the spring of 1892. The lighthouse was built, complete with two separate fog steam whistles, in case one of them malfunctioned. Once the lighthouse and the fog whistle systems were in place, work on the other outbuildings began. Next on the list to construct were the oil storage building, a barn, a well building, and most importantly, a two-seater outhouse. Tracks were then built to allow movement of supplies from the docks to the keeper's home and the fog signal building. The tower of the lighthouse housed a red fourth order Fresnel lens. Now completed, the lighthouse began its service to navigation in 1892. In 1894, the barn was renovated and converted into a home for the assistant keeper. After 64 years of service, and upon the completion of the Lansing Shoal Light, Squaw Island was deactivated. The last keeper at the light was Owen McCauley, who then transferred to the light in St. Joseph. The Gothic styled light is now privately owned and in the process of renovation.

Directions:

Squaw Island is located northwest of Beaver Island in Lake Michigan. The light can only be seen from a boat or a plane. We took Island Hoppers Charters out of Beaver Island. The web site is www.islandhopper.beaverisland.net.

GPS Waypoints:

45° 8393N
085° 5881W

Attractions and Events

Contacts:

Beaver Island Boat Company
www.bibc.com

Island Airways
www.islandairways.com

Island Hopper Charters
www.islandhopper.beaverisland.net

Beaver Island Chamber of Commerce
www.beaverisland.org

Charlevoix Area Chamber of Commerce
www.charlevoix.org

Mackinac Seaplane Tours
www.mackinacseaplanes.com

27.) Lansing Shoal Light

The Lansing Shoal presented real problems for ships heading to the north ports in Michigan and Wisconsin. With an increase in shipping, it was obvious that some type of identification marker was needed at this spot. In 1900, Lightship LV55, which had been stationed at Simmons Reef, was moved to the shoal until funding for a more permanent structure could be secured. A request for the necessary funding was made in 1908. Congress, however, did not act on the request. As a result, LV55 served her position well until the end of 1920, when it was determined that the ships hull was beyond repair. Another lightship that was being used elsewhere, LV98, was transferred to Lansing Shoal. One drawback to this move was that the lightship had to wait until the ice was almost completely gone. In the meantime, ships were forced to navigate around the shoal on their own. This problem once again reinforced the need for a permanent structure on the shoal. Congress finally approved the funding for the Lansing Shoal Light in 1926. Construction started in 1927 and finished in October 1928. Once the light was finished, LV98 returned to relief duty. Lansing Shoal's tower stands 59 feet tall and was originally outfitted with a third order Fresnel lens. Interior finish work and a radio beacon were installed in 1929. Lansing Shoal Light is still an active aid to navigation. The original third order lens is now on display at the Lansing State Museum, in Lansing Michigan. After only 48 years of active duty, the keepers left Lansing Shoal when it was automated in 1976.

Directions:

Lansing Shoal is located in Lake Michigan and can be seen by boat or plane only. We took Island Hoppers Charters out of Beaver Island. The web site is www.islandhopper.beaverisland.net. Shepler's Ferry occasionally tours this light. The web site is www.sheplersferry.com.

GPS Waypoints:

45° 9034N
085° 5616W

Attractions and Events

Contacts:

Beaver Island Boat Company
www.bibc.com

Island Airways
www.islandairways.com

Island Hopper Charters
www.islandhopper.beaverisland.net

Beaver Island Chamber of Commerce
www.beaverisland.org

Charlevoix Area Chamber of Commerce
www.charlevoix.org

Mackinac Seaplane Tours
www.mackinacseaplanes.com

Greater Mackinaw Area Chamber of Commerce
www.mackinawchamber.com

28.) Skillagalee Island Light

Skillagalee Island is located south of Grays Reef. Also known as Ile Aux Gallets, Island of Pebbles, it represents a distinct navigational hazard. The island itself is not much larger than the light that warns approaching vessels. Under the surface however, shoals extend out over 1.5 miles to the east and .5 miles to the northwest. As you can imagine, without the convenience of modern day electronics, Skillagalee claimed many victims on her shoals. The first light established on the island was built in 1851. The light was very difficult to maintain primarily from the beatings it took from Lake Michigan. The light was often damaged and in need of repairs. After only 15 years the tower had been so damaged that it needed to be rebuilt. A new tower, complete with a third order Fresnel lens, a keeper's home, and a fog signal building were built. Unfortunately, by 1888, the tower again had to be replaced. This time the 58 – foot tower, with a fourth order Fresnel lens, was attached to the keeper's home. In 1890, the fog signal was upgraded with more modern equipment. Automation arrived at Skillagalee in 1969. With no crew needed to run the light, all buildings were torn down.

Directions:

Skillagalee Island is located in Lake Michigan and can only be seen from a boat or plane. We took Island Hopper Charters out of Beaver Island. The web site is www.islandhopper.beaverisland.net.

GPS Waypoints:

45° 6772N
085° 1716W

Attractions and Events

Contacts:

Beaver Island Boat Company
www.bibc.com

Island Airways
www.islandairways.com

Island Hopper Charters
www.islandhopper.beaverisland.net

Beaver Island Chamber of Commerce
www.beaverisland.org

Charlevoix Area Chamber of Commerce
www.charlevoix.org

Mackinac Seaplane Tours
www.mackinacseaplanes.com

Greater Mackinaw Area Chamber of Commerce
www.mackinawchamber.com

Shepler's Ferry
www.sheplersferry.com

29.) Gray's Reef Light

The need for a light at Gray's Reef was no less important than any other offshore light. Navigating from the south ports through the Straits, or positioning for the Manitou Passage was a virtual obstacle course consisting of shoals and reefs. Congress approved funding for the placement of a lightship at Gray's Reef in 1899. The Lightship LV57 served honorably at the reef until declared unfit for service in 1923. The 1924 shipping season saw lightship LV103 stationed at Gray's Reef. Lightship LV103 served at the reef through the 1927 shipping season. For the 1928 shipping season, LV56, which had been at White Shoal moved to her new location at Gray's Reef. This move was short lived, lasting just one year. In 1929, LV103 returned to her previous position on the reef until her replacement, LV99 arrived from Poe Reef. Demands from larger ships and for safer passage moved Congress to approve funding for a permanent light on the reef in 1934. Now a familiar mode of operation, the crib construction began on the mainland. Gray's Reef crib work began in St. Ignace in 1934. Once the crib was complete, it was towed out to Gray's Reef. Work continued at the reef and in St. Ignace through 1935. Finally, in 1936, Gray's Reef Light, complete with a red 3.5 order Fresnel lens was complete. With the new light now operational, LV99 was no longer needed. A radio beacon was added to the light in 1937. Two years later, 1939, the Coast Guard assumed control of the light. When automation arrived to Gray's Reef in 1976, the crew was no longer needed.

Directions:

Gray's Reef is located in Lake Michigan and can only be seen from a boat or plane. We took Island Hopper Charters out of Beaver Island. The web site is www.islandhopper.beaverisland.net. Shepler's Ferry also tours this light. The web site is www.sheplersferry.com.

GPS Waypoints:

45° 7656N
085° 1542W

Attractions and Events

Contacts:

Beaver Island Boat Company
www.bibc.com

Island Airways
www.islandairways.com

Island Hopper Charters
www.islandhopper.beaverisland.net

Beaver Island Chamber of Commerce
www.beaverisland.org

Charlevoix Area Chamber of Commerce
www.charlevoix.org

Mackinac Seaplane Tours
www.mackinacseaplanes.com

Greater Mackinaw Area Chamber of Commerce
www.mackinawchamber.com

Shepler's Ferry
www.sheplersferry.com

30.) White Shoal Light

As the shipping traffic on the Great Lakes increased, and the boats grew larger in size, the light on Waugoshance Shoal became less of a factor. With these new changes it became necessary to mark White Shoal. The White Shoal Light led to the demise of the Waugoshance Shoal Light. Until a permanent light could be completed at White Shoal, a lightship took up the position. Lightship LV56 arrived at White Shoal and served faithfully until 1910. Work on the permanent light began in 1908 and would prove difficult and time consuming. The crib was constructed on shore at St. Ignace and then towed to the shoal. Construction on the tower began in the spring of 1909. Workers toiled all summer until the end of the season. Construction began again as workers arrived at the beginning of the 1910 shipping season. After three years of work, the White Shoal Light was seen for the first time, in September 1910. Inside the tower, a very large and powerful second order Fresnel lens lit up the sky. Lightship LV56 soon left for her new assignment at North Manitou Shoal. An experiment to warn ships during foggy conditions was tried in 1911. A submarine bell was submerged in the water .75 mile from the light. It was thought that the vibrations from the bell, traveling through the water, would warn on-coming ships in bad weather quicker than they could hear a fog signal from the shoal light. This experiment never matched expectations and was abandoned in 1914. In 1976, the White Shoal Light was automated. The Coast Guard did the familiar "candy cane" paint job of White Shoal Light in 1990.

Directions:

The White Shoal Light is located in Lake Michigan and can be seen best by boat or plane. We took Island Hopper Charters out of Beaver Island. The web site is www.islandhopper.beaverisland.net. We have also viewed this light aboard Shepler's Ferry. The web site is www.sheplersferry.com.

GPS Waypoints:

45° 8417N
085° 1349W

Attractions and Events

Contacts:

Beaver Island Boat Company
www.bibc.com

Island Airways
www.islandairways.com

Island Hopper Charters
www.islandhopper.beaverisland.net

Beaver Island Chamber of Commerce
www.beaverisland.org

Charlevoix Area Chamber of Commerce
www.charlevoix.org

Mackinac Seaplane Tours
www.mackinacseaplanes.com

Greater Mackinaw Area Chamber of Commerce
www.mackinawchamber.com

Shepler's Ferry
www.sheplersferry.com

31.) Waugoshance Shoal Light

There were a large number of ships that had the misfortune of going aground on this shoal prior to the completion of the Waugoshance Shoal Light. The first attempt to aid navigators came in the form of a lightship in 1832, named *Lois McLane*. The process of building this light began on St. Helena Island in 1850. The crib was constructed on St. Helena and then towed to the shoal where it was sunk. The tower of the Waugoshance Shoal Light is 76 feet tall. The tower was topped with the seldom used "bird cage" and the light was derived from a fourth order Fresnel lens. Construction on the light was finished in 1851. Harsh Lake Michigan winters forced repairs to be made on the crib after only 14 years. To better combat these conditions, it was decided to encase the light in iron. The ironwork was completed in the fall of 1883. Once again, in 1896, it became apparent that the crib would need to be repaired. In the meantime, larger ships were being used and their travels took them further away from the shoal. As it turns out, White Shoal was built in 1912 to accommodate the large ship's routes, which sealed the fate of Waugoshance Shoal. In 1912, the light was deactivated. There are two other interesting items concerning Waugoshance Shoal Light. First is that the light was used as target practice for World War II Bombers. Visitors who have seen this light up close have no doubt observed the effects of a direct hit. Secondly, it is said that the ghost of keeper John Herman haunts this light. Mr. Herman died as the result of a fall from the lighthouse in 1894.

Directions:

The Waugoshance Light is located in Lake Michigan and can be seen best by boat or plane. We took Island Hopper Charters out of Beaver Island. The web site is www.islandhopper.beaverisland.net. We have also viewed this light aboard Shepler's Ferry. The web site is www.sheplersferry.com.

GPS Waypoints:

45° 8101N
085° 1324W

Attractions and Events

Contacts:

Beaver Island Boat Company
www.bibc.com

Island Airways
www.islandairways.com

Island Hopper Charters
www.islandhopper.beaverisland.net

Beaver Island Chamber of Commerce
www.beaverisland.org

Charlevoix Area Chamber of Commerce
www.charlevoix.org

Mackinac Seaplane Tours
www.mackinacseaplanes.com

Greater Mackinaw Area Chamber of Commerce
www.mackinawchamber.com

Shepler's Ferry
www.sheplersferry.com

32.) McGulpin's Point Light

In the mid 1800's, ships traversing the Straits of Mackinac increased dramatically. The light on Waugoshance Shoal helped captains position themselves for the Straits, but once the sun went down, they were literally in the dark. A call soon was heard from the shipping industry to build a lighthouse within the Straits. A formal request for funding was made in 1854. A total of $6,000 was granted for the construction of a lighthouse and fog bell. For some reason that the history books fail to mention, construction did not begin. In fact, by the time plans were to begin, the allocation had expired. A new request was made for the necessary funding and ultimately granted in 1866. Finally, after 15 years, McGulpin's Point was established in 1869. The delay in construction proved to be a costly error. Once finished in 1869, the new cost for building the light was significantly higher, coming in at $20,000. The lighthouse was a combination dwelling and tower. Similar to the gothic style, the dwelling was two stories. The lighthouse tower housed a 3.5 order Fresnel lens. McGulpin's Point had one special light keeper in James Davenport. Mr. Davenport tended this light for 27 consecutive years. When construction began on a light at Mackinac Point, the days were numbered for this light. Construction was finished on Mackinac Point Light in 1892. The McGulpin's Point Lighthouse was deactivated in 1906. Mr. Davenport transferred to Old Mission Point Lighthouse where he served until 1917, when he then retired.

Scenic Route:

From Petoskey return to US31 and turn left. Go 2.6 miles turn left on M-119. Go 7.1 miles turn right. Go 15.5 miles turn right on Sturgeon Bay. (M-119 ends in Cross City where it turns to Lakeshore.) Go 4.4 miles turn left on M-81. Go 1.8 miles turn right. Go 1.9 miles turn left. Go 3.7 miles turn right. Go 3.7 miles turn left. Go 1 mile to yield sign continue straight on Headlands. Go 0.4 miles light is on the right. Please show respect, this is private property.

GPS Waypoints:

45° 47.232N
084° 46.428W

Direct Route:

From the corner of Nicolet and Center in Mackinaw City, take Center west 2 miles. Turn right on Headlands and go 0.4 miles. The light is on private property to the right.

Attractions and Events

Museums:
>*Colonial Michilimackinac*
>>231-436-5563
>
>*Mill Creek*
>>www.mackinacparks.com
>>231-436-7301

Points of Interest:
>*Garlyn Zoological Park*
>>www.garlynzoo.com
>
>*Animal Tracks Adventure Golf*
>>231-436-5597
>
>*Romanik's Ranch*
>>www.romaniksranch.com
>
>*Shepler's Lighthouse Cruises*
>>www.sheplersferry.com
>
>*Mackinac Island & Fort Mackinac*
>>www.mackinacparts.com

Fairs & Festivals:
>**January**
>>**Mackinaw City Winterfest**
>>**Annual Snow Ball**
>
>**February**
>>**The Mackinaw Mush**
>>**Grand Prix on Ice**
>
>**May**
>>**Fort Michilimackinac Historical Re-enactment**
>>**Memorial Day Parade and Fireworks**
>
>**June**
>>**Lilac Festival**
>>**Mackinaw Kite Festival**
>>**Mackinaw Art Fair**
>>**Straits Area Antique Autoshow**
>
>**July**
>>**4th of July Celebration**
>
>**August**
>>**War of 1812 Re-enactment**
>>**International Ironworkers Festival**
>
>**September**
>>**Labor Day Bridge Walk**
>>**Hopps of Fun – A Festival of Beer and Wine**

Contacts:
>**Greater Mackinaw Area Chamber of Commerce**
>>www.mackinawchamber.com
>>888-455-8100
>
>**Shepler's Ferry**
>>www.sheplersferry.com
>>800-828-6157
>
>**Mackinac Seaplane Tours**
>>www.mackinacseaplanes.com
>>906-632-9746

Index

Index

Index

Coming Soon

The second of the series, *The Ultimate Guide to East Michigan Lighthouses*, is scheduled for release in the summer of 2006. The final book of the series, *The Ultimate Guide to Upper Michigan Lighthouses*, is planned for release in the spring of 2008.

Visit our web site www.lighthousecentral.com, often for further updates.

Please remember that high quality photographs of all lighthouses appearing on the web site can be purchased. Keep in mind; all sales made through the web site entitle the buyer to designate a portion of the proceeds to the preservation group of their choice. All of our books can be purchased via the web site as well.

Resources

Seeing the Light
    www.terrypepper.com

Lighthouse Digest
    www.lighthousedigest.com

Night Beacon Lighthouses
    www.nightbeacon.com

Michigan Lighthouses
    www.unc.edu/~rowlett/lighthouse/mi.htm

Clarke Historical Library

Central Michigan University

The Lighthouse Directory

National Parks Service

National Lighthouse Museum

Flint Journal

Bay City Times

Lighthouses of the Great Lakes
    www.usalights.com

U. S. Coast Guard Historian
    www.michiganlights.com

History of the Great Lakes
    www.lightstations.com

Lighthouse Friends
    www.lighthousefriends.com
    www.boatnerd.com

Bugs Publishing, LLC

8524 Monroe Rd. | Durand, MI 48429 | (810) 938-3800

REFER-A-FRIEND
BOOK ORDER

BILLING INFO.

Name:

Street Address:

City: _____ State: _____ Zip: _____

Phone:

Please make checks payable to Bugs Publishing, LLC

SHIPPING INFORMATION ❏ *Same as billing* ❏ *Gift*

Name:

Attn:

Street Address:

City: _____ State: _____ Zip: _____

Phone:

QTY:	DESCRIPTION	UNIT PRICE	LINE TOTAL
	The Ultimate Guide to **West** Michigan Lighthouses	$16.95	
	The Ultimate Guide to **East** Michigan Lighthouses	$18.95	

HELP SUPPORT LIGHTHOUSE PRESERVATION

In an effort to help support the preservation of existing lighthouses, a portion of proceeds will be donated to the Lighthouse Preservation Society of your choice (indicate choice here):

Shipping ($3.50 per book)	
Subtotal	
MI Sales Tax (6%)	
TOTAL	

For book titles and pricing refer to www.lighthousecentral.com or call (810) 938-3800

1. *To complete your order, please complete this form and send to the address at the top of the form. **Don't forget to include your check or money order for the total amount due.***

2. *Please allow 4 to 6 weeks for delivery*

3. *Returned checks will be assessed a $30.00 returned check fee.*

4. *Orders will not be processed until check clears and any applicable fees have been paid.*

REFERRED BY (Name):

Address:

City, State, Zip:

Phone:

Email:

$2.00 OFF
NEXT BOOK

One coupon per book. Cannot be combined with any other discount offer.

www.lighthousecentral.com

South Manitou Island
Lighthouse

Bugs Publishing, LLC

8524 Monroe Rd. | Durand, MI 48429 | (810) 938-3800

BOOK ORDER

Billing Info.

Name:

Street Address:

City: State: Zip:

Phone:

Please make checks payable to Bugs Publishing, LLC

Shipping Information ❑ *Same as billing* ❑ *Gift*

Name:

Attn:

Street Address:

City: State: Zip:

Phone:

QTY:	DESCRIPTION	UNIT PRICE	LINE TOTAL
	The Ultimate Guide to **West** Michigan Lighthouses	$16.95	
	The Ultimate Guide to **East** Michigan Lighthouses	$18.95	

Shipping ($3.50 per book)	
Subtotal	
MI Sales Tax (6%)	
TOTAL	

HELP SUPPORT LIGHTHOUSE PRESERVATION

In an effort to help support the preservation of existing lighthouses, a portion of proceeds will be donated to the Lighthouse Preservation Society of your choice (indicate choice here):

For additional book titles and pricing refer to www.lighthousecentral.com or call (810) 938-3800

1. To complete your order, please complete this form and send to the address at the top of the form. **Don't forget to include your check or money order for the total amount due.**

2. Please allow 4 to 6 weeks for delivery

3. Returned checks will be assessed a $30.00 returned check fee.

4. Orders will not be processed until check clears and any applicable fees have been paid.

High-quality photographs are available for purchase through our web site, www.lighthousecentral.com.

A portion of the proceeds from all Internet sales is donated to a preservation group of the buyer's choice.